TEACHING
ELEMENTARY
SOCIAL STUDIES

TEACHING
ELEMENTARY
SOCIAL STUDIES

Theodore Kaltsounis

parker publishing company, inc.   west nyack, n.y.

To *Sophia* and *George*
and especially
to *Maria*

A Word from the Author About This Book

This book is directed to experienced elementary school teachers and their adminstrators. As such, it is direct and practical. Redundant and vague theoretical statements are avoided. One of the main features of this book is that it is not limited to the descriptions of ideal situations. It takes the teacher from where he is and gradually leads him into the ideal situation. The teacher is advised not only what to do, but how to do it. New approaches and teaching strategies are illustrated throughout with actual teaching incidents.

The author feels that some new programs are reluctantly received by teachers because they are almost entirely different from traditional programs. The approach of this book is a more practical and realistic one. Instead of asking teachers to reject what they have been doing all along, it asks them to incorporate the new trends within the old framework. In other words, the teacher is given guidelines with which to bridge from the old social studies to the new.

The book is divided into four parts. In the first (Chapter 1), the objectives of social studies are defined in behavioral terms. An appeal is made to the teachers to reject objectives in the form of vague verbal statements. In the second part (Chapters 2, 3, and 4), the author deals with guidelines which provide structure and unity to the social studies curriculum throughout the grades. Also, a model program is provided for the six grades of the elementary school. This program is based on new developments and has enough flexibility to allow for adaptations at the local level. The third part (Chapters 5, 6, 7, and 8) deals with planning for instruction and the various teaching resources. Part four (Chapter 9) is concerned with the evaluation of pupil progress as well as the evaluation of social studies programs. The book ends with an additional chapter (Chapter 10) addressed directly to administrators and teachers covering several specific approaches that could make the difference between a good and a poor social studies program.

Teachers appear to welcome the new directions in this subject area but not without apprehensions. Mainly, they feel inadequate in the social sciences and recognize the need to acquire proficiency in the new teaching strategies. This book should assist elementary school teachers in overcoming these apprehensions and improve their teaching of social studies by bringing the new trends to the classroom.

Theodore Kaltsounis

Contents

9

TEACHING
ELEMENTARY
SOCIAL STUDIES

1

Developing Key Objectives for Social Studies

The educational world has started to pay close attention to the social studies, whereas for a time, science and mathematics were in the forefront.

The reasons for the switch towards the social studies, or towards a balance at least, are many: The competition between the United States and the Soviet Union in the development of warfare materials, which forced a priority for technological knowledge and skill has decreased somewhat. Both parties accepted the principle of coexistence and there is an increasing tendency towards cooperation. The awakening of the minority groups in this country has shaken the social equilibrium and generated an atmosphere of crisis. The relationships between management and labor have become very complex and often issues are raised which are based on narrow interests without any regard for the general welfare. City life has become very complicated and difficult and the role of federal and state governments in the everyday affairs of citizens has increased.

The American society is a multigroup society in which people play many and different roles. The core of common values continues to diminish and the number of those who dispute what were once virtually sacred beliefs is increasing. Within all this confusion, the teacher of social studies faces a dilemma as to her role and purpose in teaching about human relationships.

The purpose of this chapter is to help teachers formulate the objectives in social studies. A specific method is recommended by means of which a teacher may arrive at realistic objectives through a planned process.

The description of this process must begin with the understanding that by educational objectives we mean desirable changes in behavior, and that the major function of all education is understood to be the development of good citizens. Following these assumptions, lists of behavioral characteristics of good citizens can be developed.

Which of these characteristics are the responsibility of social studies instruction? An attempt is made to answer this question by referring to the specific function of the social studies. The result is a list of common objectives for the elementary school. Most important among these objectives are concepts and generalizations, but teachers are not clear as to what they are, what the difference is between them, and how they are developed. An attempt is made in this chapter to clear the confusion in regard to concepts and generalizations.

Social studies objectives listed in the various teacher aids are usually stated in general terms, and must be applied in specific cases with the discretion of the individual teacher paramount. Examples are cited to illustrate this point.

In the last parts of the chapter, the importance of the concept of democracy and the skills related to problem solving are stressed.

Objectives should be changes in behavior

In order for someone to understand the objectives of social studies, or any objectives, he needs to have a general philosophy of learning. The best definition of learning which psychologists have formulated is that it is change in behavior. We know that a child has learned something only if his behavior has changed in an observable manner. Verbalization only is not an adequate indication that a child has learned.

Benjamin S. Bloom and his associates in their book *Taxonomy of*

Educational Objectives[1] identify three domains in the individual which are subject to change through learning experiences. These are the cognitive, the affective, and the psychomotor domains.

Changes in the *cognitive domain* take place when the individual becomes capable of recalling or recognizing knowledge or when he has developed intellectual abilities and skills with which to evaluate and use the knowledge which he acquires. Changes in the *affective domain* are changes in interests, attitudes, and values as well as the development of appreciations and adequate adjustment. The third domain involves changes in the manipulative or motor-skill area.

The "old school" was only concerned about the development of the cognitive domain and largely ignored the other two. While the cognitive domain still continues to be a primary concern for the new school as well, the overall purpose of modern education is to develop the total individual. All three domains are interrelated and the development of any one of them is affected by the status of the other two.

For example, the undertaking of deliberate changes in the cognitive domain will meet with difficulties when the affective domain is disturbed or when health and vigor are impaired. It must also be considered that the ultimate goal of education is good citizenship which implies the development of men of commitment and action as well as men who are knowledgeable.

The behavioral characteristics of a good citizen

Since the development of good citizens is the ultimate and overall purpose of education, the teacher should be reminded of the behavioral characteristics of good citizens. It is out of these characteristics that the objectives of social studies will emerge.

The most accepted list of the behavioral characteristics of the good citizen is found in *The Purpose of Education in American Democracy*, a publication of the Educational Policies Commission of the National Education Association and the American Association of School Administrators. These purposes are classified in four categories as follows:

A. The Objectives of Self-Realization
   1. *The Inquiring Mind*. The educated person has an appetite for learning.

---

[1] Benjamin S. Bloom, ed. *Taxonomy of Educational Objectives, Handbook I: Cognitive Domain* (New York: David McKay Co., Inc., 1956).

2. *Speech.* The educated person speaks the mother tongue clearly.

3. *Reading.* The educated person reads the mother tongue efficiently.

4. *Writing.* The educated person writes the mother tongue effectively.

5. *Number.* The educated person solves his problems of counting and calculating.

6. *Sight and Hearing.* The educated person is skilled in listening and observing.

7. *Health Knowledge.* The educated person understands the basic facts concerning health and disease.

8. *Health Habits.* The educated person protects his own health and that of his dependents.

9. *Public Health.* The educated person works to improve the health of the community.

10. *Recreation.* The educated person is a participant and spectator in many sports and other pastimes.

11. *Intellectual Interests.* The educated person has mental resources for the use of leisure.

12. *Esthetic Interests.* The educated person appreciates beauty.

13. *Character.* The educated person gives responsible direction to his own life.

B. The Objectives of Human Relationship

1. *Respect for Humanity.* The educated person puts human relationships first.

2. *Friendships.* The educated person enjoys a rich, sincere, and varied social life.

3. *Cooperation.* The educated person can work and play with others.

4. *Courtesy.* The educated person observes the amenities of social behavior.

5. *Appreciation of the Home.* The educated person appreciates the family as a social institution.

6. *Conservation of the Home.* The educated person conserves family ideals.

7. *Homemaking.* The educated person is skilled in homemaking.

8. *Democracy in the Home.* The educated person maintains democratic family relationships.

C. The Objectives of Economic Efficiency

1. *Work.* The educated producer knows the satisfaction of good workmanship.
2. *Occupational Information.* The educated producer understands the requirements and opportunities for various jobs.
3. *Occupational Choice.* The educated producer has selected his occupation.
4. *Occupational Efficiency.* The educated producer succeeds in his chosen vocation.
5. *Occupational Adjustment.* The educated producer maintains and improves his efficiency.
6. *Occupational Appreciation.* The educated producer appreciates the social value of his work.
7. *Personal Economics.* The educated consumer plans the economics of his own life.
8. *Consumer Judgment.* The educated consumer develops standards for guiding his expenditures.
9. *Efficiency in Buying.* The educated consumer is an informed and skillful buyer.
10. *Consumer Protection.* The educated consumer takes appropriate measures to safeguard his interests.

D. The Objectives of Civic Responsibility

1. *Social Justice.* The educated citizen is sensitive to the disparities of human circumstance.
2. *Social Activity.* The educated citizen acts to correct unsatisfactory conditions.
3. *Social Understanding.* The educated citizen seeks to understand social structures and social processes.
4. *Critical Judgment.* The educated citizen has defenses against propaganda.
5. *Tolerance.* The educated citizen respects honest differences of opinion.
6. *Conservation.* The educated citizen has a regard for the nation's resources.
7. *Social Applications of Science.* The educated citizen measures scientific advance by its contribution to the general welfare.

8. *World Citizenship.* The educated citizen is a cooperating member of the world community.
9. *Law Observance.* The educated citizen respects the law.
10. *Economic Literacy.* The educated citizen is economically literate.
11. *Political Citizenship.* The educated citizen accepts his civic duties.
12. *Devotion to Democracy.* The educated citizen acts upon an unswerving loyalty to democratic ideals.[2]

The development of the objectives of the last three major categories is largely the task of social studies.

A second set of objectives of education reported by Donald W. Robinson is oriented even more towards the social studies. Dr. Robinson, Director of the Civic Education Project of the National Council for the Social Studies, has projected the following twelve basic behaviors as the goals for the education of citizens:

1. A general all around concern for information and skills.
2. A specific concern for knowing about the impact of science on civilization.
3. Concern for knowing about the economic issues that affect our lives.
4. Helping the student to make value judgments that will enable him to function constructively in a changing world.
5. Teaching him that we live in an open-ended world and that he must be receptive to new things, new ideas, and new processes of living.
6. Helping him to develop a set of principles consistent with his democratic heritage, and teaching him to apply them conscientiously in his daily living.
7. A good citizen should be committed to both liberty of the individual and equality of rights for all as provided by the Constitution of the United States.
8. A good citizen is committed to his responsibility to participate in decision making.
9. A good citizen should feel committed to pride in the achievements of the United States at the same time that he appreciates

[2] Educational Policies Commission, *The Purposes of Education in American Democracy.* (Washington, D.C.: Educational Policies Commission of National Education Association and the American Association of School Administrators, 1938).

the contributions to civilization of other peoples throughout the world.

10. The good citizen should feel the importance of the creative arts to sensitize himself to human experience and to develop the uniqueness of his personality.

11. A good citizen must be committed to the necessity of compassion for other human beings and must be sensitive to their needs, their feelings, and their aspirations.

12. A good citizen must appreciate and feel committed to the proposition that a continuation of human existence depends upon the reduction of national rivalries, and must work for international cooperation and order.[3]

The specific function of social studies

As it was already suggested, social studies objectives should emerge from and be consistent with the objectives of education in general. In a democracy, the purpose of general education is to create and sustain an enlightened and good citizenry. Every individual should be adequately informed about his social and physical environments and he should have his individual capacities developed to the point where he can function successfully within these environments. Contributions towards improving both the social and physical environments are expected from those demonstrating higher capacities.

Promoting good citizenship, therefore, is an end cooperatively sought in all subjects and school activities, and social studies plays only a part which is dictated by its specific function. Social studies education and citizenship education are not synonymous and they should not be used as such.

It is necessary to explicitly state the specific function of social studies in order that it may be used as a guide in the identification of those objectives of education which ought to be the focus of social studies instruction.

The specific function of social studies is to inform the young about the various kinds of human relationships, and to provide opportunities through which the future citizens will develop those capacities and qualities necessary for their successful participation in human relationships. The development of all other attributes of a good citizen,

---

[3] Donald W. Robinson, "Educating Citizens for the 21st Century," *Civic Leader*, Vol. 35 (May 16, 1966) pp. 1–4.

such as the ability to read and write, to understand physical phenomena, and to manipulate numbers, is the responsibility of other subjects.

Teachers who wish to develop and teach a sound social studies curriculum need to keep this specific function of social studies in mind so that they can avoid leading themselves astray through interesting, but unrelated activities. A specific teacher from the maple syrup countryside reported that she spends two months out of the year studying the process of maple syrup. Her justification for doing this was not the development of economic concepts but that the children enjoyed doing what everyone in the community was doing. Taking into consideration the criterion for the selection of this rather prolonged activity, it is doubtful whether it was within the specific function of social studies. It might be true that the children developed certain social skills while involved in this activity, but the same social skills could have been developed just as well through the study of genuine and structured social studies content selected with the assistance of strong objectives.

The most common objectives of elementary social studies

What, then, are the common objectives for elementary school social studies? It should be pointed out that as far as the general objectives of social studies are concerned, there is no difference between the elementary and the secondary levels. The difference lies only in the approach for reaching the objectives due to the maturity level of the pupils.

The elementary school social studies objectives are usually found in the state courses of study, the various curriculum guides, and the textbooks. A recent study done with the intent of identifying the most common elementary school social studies objectives was reported by Clarence Samford.[4] Dr. Samford reviewed current statements of objectives in fifteen state courses of study, fifteen school system curriculum guides, fifteen periodical articles, and five social studies methods textbooks. As a result, he compiled a list of objectives which were then classified in a way which appears to reflect closely the three domains of the individual as defined earlier in this chapter. Included in the list are:

---

[4] Clarence D. Samford, "Can Social Studies Objectives Be Accomplished with Present Day Textbooks?" *The Social Studies*, Vol. 45 (April 1954) pp. 134–137.

A. Objectives related to acquiring social studies information:

1. Knowledge of democracy and the manner in which it functions.
2. Understanding of social, economic, and political concepts starting with the community and extending into a world setting.
3. Information dealing with contemporary affairs.
4. Acquisition of sound economic, political and social ideas.
5. Gaining of an adequate social studies vocabulary.
6. Comprehensive knowledge of the history and traditions of our own country.
7. Learning the basic facts of consumer education.
8. Strengthening and enriching personality.
9. Securing vocational education.
10. Deriving a suitable background for other areas in the curriculum.
11. Stressing the importance of conservation education.

B. Objectives related to acquiring social studies skills:

1. Ability to make use of table of contents, index, maps, charts, graphs, dictionary, encyclopedia, atlas, almanacs, selected cartoons, and other resource tools.
2. Developing powers of critical thinking and independent judgment.
3. Participation in group discussion.
4. Effective presentation of oral reports.
5. Application of social studies information to practical situations.
6. Working in groups within the classroom.
7. Using community resources as an aid to the learning of social studies.
8. Enlarging opportunities for growth in reading.
9. Working on committees and in projects designed to help the local community and/or larger group.
10. Relying upon audio-visual aids as a means of enlarging social studies concepts.
11. Giving opportunity to learn parliamentary procedures.
12. Development of leadership.
13. Collecting data.
14. Application of the rules of effective study.

C. Objectives related to acquiring desirable social studies attitudes:

1. Respect for rights and contribution of others regardless of race, color, and creed.
2. Desire to participate personally in improving various groups, for example, the home, school, community, state, and nation.
3. Appreciation of the sacrifices that have gone into the making of our social order.
4. Exaltation of high social values.
5. Gaining respect for work well done.
6. Cultivation of laudable patriotism.
7. Respect for truth (accuracy).
8. Standing for high moral and spiritual values.

Though the above list of objectives was compiled more than ten years ago, a review of more recent statements reveals that there has been almost no change.

Concepts, generalizations, and conceptualization

The preceding list implies that the knowledge category of objectives includes facts, events, concepts, and generalizations. The attitudes category includes interests, dispositions, beliefs, ideals and values. The skills category includes skills of social behavior and a number of social studies skills such as map reading, graph interpretation, distinguishing between a factual report and an opinionated editorial, and others.

The meaning of these objectives is quite clear except for concepts and generalizations. Many have tried to define the terms "concept" and "generalization" but the average teacher seems confused. If one were to make a list of everything that is labeled in the various syllabi as concepts and everything that is labeled as generalizations and compare them, he would discover that what are called concepts in one source are called generalizations in another.

At a time in which conceptualization is so much in the forefront, it is very necessary to point out the difference between a concept and a generalization and suggest the possible source of confusion.

A concept is a word or phrase which denotes a group of objects or ideas with common characteristics. When we see a mountain we recognize it and we call it as such in spite of the fact that there are no two mountains exactly alike. The word mountain refers to something which is concrete—one can see it, touch it, walk on it. Concepts about which we become aware through our senses are usually known as tangible concepts. Words such as cooperation, tolerance, democracy, and the like are known as intangible concepts. They cannot be experienced through the senses. The intangible concepts are more difficult to teach and most of the concepts in social studies are of this type.

A generalization is a statement of a relationship with broad applicability. The statements "when the demand for housing increases rent increases," and "revolutions bring about sweeping changes in the old social order" are definitely statements of relationship, but this is not enough to make them generalizations. In order for these statements of relationship to be generalizations, they must meet the criterion of broad applicability. Does the rent go up everywhere when the demand for housing goes up? Did all the revolutions in the past and all around the world bring sweeping changes in the old social order? If the answers to these two questions are "yes," the above statements of relationship are generalizations.

There are weak and strong generalizations depending upon the broadness of the applicability of the relationship. Let us suppose that we have randomly selected one hundred places around the world to check if rent really increases with the increase in the demand for housing. If in all of these hundred places this really did happen, the generalization is very strong. The smaller the number of cases in which the relationship existed, the weaker the generalization.

What confuses concepts with generalizations is the process of developing them. To enable the youngsters to form a generalization, we make them aware of its broad application by bringing to their attention as many instances of application as possible. Then the children themselves arrive at the conclusion that this relationship is a generalization. In other words, they discover the generalization by putting together specific instances.

In forming concepts, a similar process of generalizing takes place. When a youngster is faced with an object or idea, he must decide in what category to classify it and give it a name. So, when the youngster sees an apple he puts together a number of specifics—the color, the texture, a feeling of the taste, the shape. On the basis of these specifics he reaches a conclusion that the object is an apple. In other words, on the basis of a number of specific impressions, the child generalizes about the object.

The process of forming or discovering concepts and generalizations through an analysis of the specifics involved is the method of conceptualization. All trends indicate that it is a better method of teaching social studies.

A need for interpretation of the objectives

It is not enough for a group of teachers or a particular teacher to decide upon a list of general objectives. Each one of these objectives has to be applied so as to elicit specific behaviors appropriate for the maturity level of the child. Unless this is done, the objectives fail to function as guides for the selection of content and the teacher floats aimlessly, incapable of making sound selections from the vast amount of content which exists. Furthermore, evaluation becomes impossible. Following are some illustrations of interpretation of objectives:

A particular teacher wished to have her third graders understand the generalization that interdependence has been a constant and important factor in human relationships everywhere. There was no one single behavior on the basis of which this teacher could ascertain that the children had developed an understanding of the generalization. She had to teach the lessons so as to bring about specific observable behaviors on the basis of which she could assume that the children understood the relationship. Some of the specific behaviors were: the ability in children to define interdependence in terms of situations in their own immediate environment; the conviction on the part of the students that interdependence is a necessity in the lives of groups of people— family, neighborhood, school, and community; the realization on the part of the students that every community and every nation needs some things from other communities and nations; the ability in children to cite situations of interdependence between communities and nations; the showing of respect for individuals who provide various kinds of services; the ability in children to elaborate some of the factors which caused interdependence to increase in the past years. Of course, the teacher's intention was not to complete the development of all these behaviors. She made a good start and took each child as far as he could go.

Another teacher was interested in having her children develop the generalization that life on earth is influenced by the earth's (global) shape, its size and its set of motions. She listed the following specific behaviors related to the generalization: the ability to explain verbally and through illustrations the phenomena of night and day and the various seasons; the ability to determine approximately the general activities of people on various parts of the earth and at specific times by referring to the globe—its motions and its relationship to the sun; the ability of the children to specify how different their needs would be if they lived in various parts of the world; an appreciation of nature's order, in spite of the fact that some phenomena are disturbing to human activities.

The number of specific behaviors to which an objective may be interpreted is not set. It depends on the nature of the objective and on the ability level of the children. Generally speaking, most of the common objectives can be interpreted to a number of behaviors ranging from the most simple to the most complex depending upon the intellectual involvement which they require.

As John Jarolimek has suggested,[5] a good guide to help teachers analyze the results of broad objectives on specific behaviors is Bloom's model.[6] Bloom and his associates break general objectives down to the following six categories of behavior:

1. Knowledge
2. Comprehension
3. Application
4. Analysis
5. Synthesis
6. Evaluation

These are ordered in terms of a hierarchy, and behaviors in each succeeding category are to some extent dependent upon an understanding of related objectives in a prior category.

The *knowledge* category includes behaviors such as the ability to recall specifics, facts, terminology and events. The *comprehension* cate-

---

[5] John Jarolimek, "The Taxonomy: Guide to Differentiated Instruction," *Social Education*, Vol. XXVI (Dec. 1962) pp. 445–447.

[6] Benjamin S. Bloom, ed., *Taxonomy of Educational Objectives, Handbook I: Cognitive Domain* (New York: David McKay Co., Inc., 1956).

gory implies that the child is capable of translating or interpreting one form of communication to another. The *application* category means that the child is capable of using what he learned in his efforts to deal with new problem situations. The category of *analysis* implies that a youngster has developed the ability to discover the parts and the organization principles of a particular communication or subject. *Synthesis* is of a higher mental level and implies that the youngster is capable of putting together the parts of a communication and creating a whole. *Evaluation* demands yet more intellectual involvement and refers to the ability of children to make judgments on the basis of internal or external criteria.

In closing this section, it should be pointed out that Bloom's ideas are highly respected among educators across the nation. It is recommended that teachers devote a few of their professional meetings to familiarize themselves with these ideas.

The elementary school and the concept of democracy

To know about democracy is not as important as to be able to live it. The term democracy denotes mainly not a body of knowledge but a way of life. The primary emphasis in the elementary school should be the development in children of democratic behaviors which involve commitments and skills. These commitments and skills cannot be developed through lectures; they are developed, instead, through actual practice and through the influence of the child's environment.

The various teachers' manuals and syllabi never fail to list objectives related to the democratic way of life, but some of the teachers' practices are not conducive to the development of these objectives. Respect for others is a very basic democratic behavior, but some teachers do not respect their own pupils. The teaching profession is probably the only profession whose members make fun of their clientele. In other professions this would probably be a violation of ethics, but too many teachers call their pupils "brats," "monsters," "stupid," and even "animals." One will not have to visit many teachers' rooms to discover this. Developing the skill of cooperation and a sense of importance through making a contribution in the life of the group is necessary. Many teachers, however, allow no other views to prevail but their own.

It is very important that teachers recognize the potentialities of children and create an atmosphere of permissiveness with responsibility in which these potentialities can develop. Many teachers bore the youngsters with textbook content far below the ability level of these youngsters. This is why many of our children lose interest in learning and withdraw that precious quality of free people, which is called curiosity.

Several years ago, a group of researchers asked 812 juniors and seniors in the high schools of Detroit to write an essay on the question, "What Does Democracy Mean to You?" These essays were then analyzed to determine if students realized that freedom is essential to the concept of democracy, and if they thought democracy means obligations just as much as it means rights. The results indicated that more than 90 percent of the students recognized freedom as a basic ingredient in the meaning of democracy. As far as the second objective of the study was concerned, the results were not as encouraging; of the total number of statements, 84.2 percent were concerned with rights while only 15.8 percent were concerned with obligations.[7] To what extent is the elementary school responsible for this situation?

Problem solving as an objective in elementary social studies

In the elementary school of the past, problem solving was usually associated with arithmetic and sometimes with science. Today it is considered to be one of the most important objectives to be achieved through the teaching of social studies as well. Textbooks on social studies methods devote a whole chapter, or a least a good portion of one, to problem solving. Curriculum guides across the nation stress the importance of this skill and suggest ways for its development. The National Council for the Social Studies considers problem solving again and again in its yearbooks and other publications. Encyclopedia articles and articles in professional journals project problem solving as a fundamental objective for social studies. In a democracy, problem solving ability is an important skill for every citizen to possess.

The importance of problem solving stems from two characteristics of social studies content. One of these characteristics is the fact that social studies content deals with human relationships, formal in our institutions, and informal in everyday social interactions. The forms

---

[7] Stanley E. Dimond, *Schools and the Development of Good Citizens* (Detroit: Wayne University Press, 1953), pp. 74–75.

of human relationships change and today they change very rapidly. This is inevitable and there are reasons for each change. Young people should be educated to see and understand these reasons for changes. If they do so, there is hope that as adults they will be willing to accept changes more readily; consequently, the cultural lag, which is of so much concern to sociologists, will be lessened. This, if it takes place, will constitute an outstanding contribution on the part of today's schools to the society of tomorrow.

The second characteristic of social studies content which demands the development of problem solving is the fact that human relationships are, so often, conflicts. Probably there was no time in history in which conflicts among people have had the dimensions which they have today. Neither was there a time when conflicts among groups of people meant the possibility of the destruction of the whole world. If people are to survive and live together in groups, small or large, they must be able to look at these conflicts with open minds and arrive at decisions which will motivate them to act in behalf of the general welfare. This is a very difficult task to accomplish. Teachers as well as other adults should start very early and keep working with zeal in order to develop these important traits in the citizens of tomorrow.

What exactly is problem solving and what is its status in the public schools?

Psychologists have done considerable research to define problem solving. All of it, however, was done under laboratory conditions and the reports were written in such technical terms that teachers have difficulty understanding them.

Two specialists in the teaching of social studies, Richard Gross and Frederick McDonald,[8] made a rather thorough survey of psychological research in order to determine whether problem solving is a process of recognizing, a process of integrating, or some kind of an "insight." They have come to the conclusion that problem solving is a complex function rather than a single unitary function.

Basically, we may think of problem solving as a series of progressive steps which a person takes when faced with a problem. These steps are:

---

[8] Richard E. Gross and Frederick J. McDonald, "The Problem Solving Approach," *Phi Delta Kappan*, Vol. 39 (March 1958), pp. 259–265.

1. Initial stage, in which a person becomes aware of a problem requiring a solution.
2. Data-gathering phase, in which the person familiarizes himself with the problem and seeks materials for solution.
3. Hypothesis formation state, in which the person formulates tentative solutions.
4. Hypothesis testing phase, in which solutions are tested.

All basic textbooks in the teaching of social studies advocate similar steps in the method of problem solving. It will be noted that these are essentially the same steps as John Dewey lists as steps in critical thinking.[9]

Since problem solving is so important, one might assume that teachers made it their basic method of instruction. This does not appear to be the case, however, as is revealed by the research which is available.

The Detroit Citizenship Study[10] is probably the only major study of its kind which dealt at length with the social studies in the elementary school. Among the eight schools used in the study, four were elementary schools. Problem solving was considered an essential skill and the investigators proposed to investigate the extent to which it was used in the classrooms. According to the director of the study, "The evidence showed that not much experience was given in the schools to thinking or problem solving. There were few examples in classes of weighing evidence or considering alternative choices. Test data also indicated a weakness in this area."[11]

The investigators identified the following three major reasons as preventing the teaching of problem solving:

1. Lack of problem solving theory on the part of the teachers.
2. Lack of know-how to develop the abilities of problem solving.
3. The insecurity on the part of many teachers with respect to the study of controversial issues in the classroom.

---

[9] John Dewey, *Democracy and Education* (New York: The Macmillan Company, 1916), p. 192.

[10] Stanley E. Dimond, *Schools and the Development of Good Citizens* (Detroit: Wayne University Press, 1953).

[11] Stanley E. Dimond, "The Detroit Citizenship Study," *Phi Delta Kappan*, Vol. 34 (Dec. 1951), p. 174.

Another study conducted in Minnesota by Paul Torrance[12] indicated that elementary school teachers fail to give the deserved attention to the development of problem solving abilities while teaching social studies. Professor Torrance based his study on J. P. Guilford's theory of mental operations which enumerates them as cognition, memory, convergent thinking, divergent thinking, and evaluation.[13] Divergent thinking and evaluation are the most important operations in the development of problem solving.

In Torrance's study, 390 elementary teachers across the state of Minnesota were asked to identify a specific unit which they taught in social studies and list the three most important objectives they meant to achieve. The objectives were then classified on the basis of the mental operations to find out the extent to which divergent thinking and evaluation were stressed.

The results were disappointing; of 1,070 objectives submitted by the teachers only nine or 0.9 percent were related to divergent thinking and five or 0.5 percent were related to evaluation. "It seems obvious," wrote Torrance, "that far too many teachers are concerned only about *familiarizing* or *acquainting* pupils with ideas, facts and concepts. Others seem to be concerned only about developing the *'right' attitude*, establishing behavioral norms. The concern for doing something with what is learned is largely lacking."[14]

Teachers will be able to involve the youngsters in problem solving and other processes which employ and reward the mind by:

1. Providing for a sound and structured curriculum;
2. Eliminating the use of one textbook as the only source;
3. Adapting the unit method of teaching which enables the youngsters to acquire knowledge and develop attitudes and skills through experience at their level;
4. Utilizing a wide range of instructional materials.

---

[12] Paul E. Torrance and Janet Ross, *Improving Social Studies Education in Minnesota* (Minneapolis: Bureau of Educational Research of the University of Minnesota, 1961), Mimeographed.

[13] J. P. Guilford, "Three Faces of Intellect," *The American Psychologist*, (August 1959), pp. 469–479.

[14] Paul E. Torrance and Janet Ross, *Improving Social Studies Education in Minnesota* (Minneapolis: Bureau of Educational Research of the University of Minnesota, 1961), Mimeographed, p. 68.

Summary

Since social studies are concerned with human relationships, the objectives of social studies are those behaviors which are considered necessary for an individual to function well in his social situations.

The common objectives of elementary school social studies are classified in three categories: knowledge, attitudes, and skills which reflect the three domains of the individual—the cognitive, the affective and psychomotor. Concepts and generalizations are included in the knowledge category and the difference between the two is not always clear. Concepts are words denoting classes of objects and ideas, while generalizations are statements of relationship with broad applicability. The process of forming concepts and generalizations inductively is called conceptualization.

Objectives are usually stated in broad terms and must be applied with discretion by the individual teacher to elicit specific behaviors appropriate for the level of a particular student or group of students.

Two of the most important objectives to be stressed in today's schools are democratic behavior and the development of problem solving ability. Both of these develop through experience and there is evidence to show that teachers do not provide enough opportunities for such experiences.

Objectives are very important because they make possible the selection of a sound curriculum and provide for a realistic process of evaluation.

Establishing Reliable Guidelines to Improve the Social Studies Curriculum

2

Establishing Reliable Guidelines to Improve the Social Studies Curriculum

In writing this chapter the author put himself in the position of a curriculum committee which is composed of classroom teachers and has as its task the development of a sound social studies program for the elementary grades. In view of the present day ferment in the social studies, there are many of these committees operating across the nation. The first job of all such committees is to establish guidelines on the basis of which they will be able to function well.

First hand observations and active participation in social studies curriculum committees suggest the following guidelines:

1. The teachers in the committee should examine their present program and identify its deficiencies. A realization of these deficiencies will motivate the teachers to do something to eliminate them. Furthermore, it will make them more receptive to the steps which follow.
2. In order for the committee to be able to take the right direc-

tion, its members should study the trends in social studies education by reviewing some of the major social studies projects recently under way across the nation.

3. Finally, based on the information in the first two steps, the teachers should provide for a sound structure in the curriculum through the use of generalizations, and eliminate trivial content and repetitions by adapting a modified version of the expanding environment approach in the organization of the program.

Awareness of deficiencies

This chapter is concerned with the curriculum of social studies. If the objectives are the blueprint for a house, the curriculum is the material with which the house will be built. A teacher cannot possibly achieve worthwhile objectives without a sound and appropriate curriculum.

Recent nation-wide surveys by Hodgson,[1] Preston,[2] Burns and Frazier,[3] Barnes,[4] and Adams,[5] reveal that the elementary social studies curriculum is similar across the nation. In the primary grades it is home, school, community helpers, pets, farm life, communication, transportation, food, shelter, clothing, and Indians. In the fourth grade it is the regions of the world from the climatic point of view, mainly how it affects the lives of people. The United States of America (sometimes Canada and Latin America as well) is the content for the fifth grade. The rest of the world, with emphasis on Europe, is taught in the sixth grade.

The teacher is cautioned, however, not to consider this uniformity of the social studies curriculum as a criterion for judging its quality. There is substantial evidence which casts serious doubts upon the valid-

---

[1] Frank M. Hodgson, "Trends in Social Studies in the Elementary School," *School and Society*, Volume 80 (September 18, 1954), pp. 85–87.

[2] Ralph C. Preston, *Teaching Social Studies in the Elementary School*, Revised Edition. (New York: Holt, Rinehart and Winston, 1962), p. 33.

[3] Richard F. Burns and Alexander Frazier, "A Survey of Elementary School Social Studies Programs," *Social Education*, Volume 21 (May 1957), pp. 202–204.

[4] D. L. Barnes, "What Are We Teaching in Social Studies and Sciences?" *Education*, Volume 81 (October 1960), pp. 121–123.

[5] Fay Adams, *Curriculum Content and Basic Materials in the Social Studies* (Los Angeles: University of Southern California, 1962).

ity of this curriculum. Dissatisfaction with the content and the organization of today's elementary school social studies program comes
from all directions. A quick review of the literature finds the authorities
in the field quite disturbed with the status quo. Alert teachers in the
field are considerably unhappy with present syllabi and textbooks and
they are frantically in search of new ideas and instructional materials.
Realization of the invalidity of the present social studies curriculum
led to a wide and feverish movement across the nation to revise it
through research and experimentation. The federal government and
other agencies and organizations are spending sizable amounts of
money to support this movement.

In this chapter the deficiencies of the present program will be
discussed first with the hope that all teachers will become concerned
and willing to dare to make changes. The second part of the chapter
contains descriptions of some of the major attempts to overcome the
deficiencies as well as suggestions for improving the present curriculum
at the classroom level.

What are the deficiencies?

A major deficiency in today's elementary social studies program
is the fact that it is lacking a basic structure. Most of the units which
are taught today are not selected on the basis of a general philosophical
framework which could tie them together. Instead, they are randomly
selected, and teachers usually stress those topics in which they are
interested without any regard to the basic generalizations in the
social sciences. Facts and events are taught in isolation rather than
as bits of evidence for the formulation of basic relationships.

A program not structured around concepts and generalizations
tends to become anti-intellectual and the children waste a lot of valuable time drawing, for instance, pictures of community helpers. "When
I take a Professor of Not-Education into a second-grade classroom
where children are drawing pictures of their Community Helper, the
Friendly Mailman," Bruce Joyce wrote recently, "I want to hide under
the table in the science corner." He goes on to say that "Whatever the
causes, the charge of anti-intellectualism seems to me to have some
merit. Many textbooks and many teachers begin with what the child
is familiar with, in accordance with the expanding horizons approach,

but they leave him right there, rather than leading him to a more sophisticated level of understanding."[6]

Another deficiency is the fact that much of the content is outdated or not based on reality. In looking at some of the units on the Netherlands, for example, one gets the impression that everyone walks around in wooden shoes. This fact is rather trivial and outdated, but one rarely finds a teacher who will not present it. At the same time the majority of teachers will say very little or nothing about the role of Holland as a member of the European Common Market or the North Atlantic Treaty Organization.

In an attempt to discover the causes for this particular deficiency one cannot overlook the apathy of many teachers. During summer school and in courses designed for the improvement of instruction, teachers do not cease to amaze this writer with their lack of knowledge on some of the world shaking international conflicts and developments. While there are some outstanding teachers in the field equipped with inspiring professional zeal, many of them find more pleasure in gossip than in the types of activities which will advance them professionally and assist in updating their education. Many of our student teachers come back from their schools disturbed, discouraged, and disappointed because they find some of the teachers' rooms to be no more than gossip centers.

On the other hand, the outdatedness of the content is the result of administrative authority coupled with indifference. Some administrators require that their teachers follow a specific set of books in spite of the fact that these books might be five, ten or even fifteen years old.

Still another deficiency is evident in the textbooks. Many have an unjustified bias which tends to distort the real nature of our society. Often children do not have both parents. Yet, all children in the social studies textbooks have a mother and a father. Few of our children are fortunate enough to live in Cape Cod colonial-type homes, but all children in our books do. By tradition, names like Papadopoulos or Suhukowa are very unpopular in our social studies textbooks. The Indians displayed great heroism in defending their land, but they are

---

[6] Bruce R. Joyce, "The Primary Grades: A Review of Textbook Materials," in: C. Benjamin Cox and Byron G. Massialas, ed., *Social Studies in the United States: A Critical Appraisal* (New York: Harcout, Brace and World, Inc., 1967), p. 27.

portrayed as savages and the "bad guys" while the whites were the "good guys."

While publishers are striving at the present to improve the content of social studies, most of the textbooks still lack quality. Looking at them from another point of view, William Rader wrote, "Most of the information presented in textbooks is descriptive rather than analytical, and the books do not give students an opportunity to review critically the information presented or to apply the techniques and concepts of social sciences."[7]

It was implied earlier that social studies in the primary grades are oversimplified and easy. The children often know the content before they formally study it. In the upper grades, however, the content is overwhelming. An attempt is made to cover various countries or regions one-by-one instead of on the basis of fundamental understandings that unify or differentiate them. This lack of a smooth flow in the sequence of content from the primary to the upper grades presents another important deficiency.

A final limitation of the present social studies program points to the fact that it is too exclusively oriented toward the United States and Europe. Knowing about one's own country is imperative, but in a world such as ours there is a need for the development of a more global concept and outlook. The present program cannot possibly achieve this to the degree to which it should.

The limitations of the current social studies curriculum quoted from Patricia Schmuck provide a very concise and clear summary:

> (1) The social studies are viewed as information children must learn; (2) the social studies do not distinguish between inquiry into values and indoctrination of values; (3) the social studies make little use of the social sciences that deal with man in his social world, that is, psychology, social psychology, anthropology and economics; and (4) too little has been expected of children; our assumptions about their learning potential have been erroneous.[8]

---

[7] William D. Rader, "The Intermediate Grades: Should Children Answer Their Own Questions?" in: C. Benjamin Cox and Byron G. Massialas, ed., *Social Studies in the United States: A Critical Appraisal* (New York: Harcourt, Brace and World, Inc., 1967), p. 43.

[8] *Ibid.*, p. 41.

Major efforts to improve the curriculum

There are several social studies curriculum projects which have gained nation-wide recognition. It is certain that none of them promises a standard curriculum for the nation. Nevertheless, each has something to offer to teachers at the local level.

The Stanford Project. Paul Hanna of Stanford University has advanced what is considered to be a very meaningful approach for the improvement of social studies. Dr. Hanna begins with the assumption that the purpose of social studies is to develop individuals who would be capable of functioning effectively in society. In turn, he recognizes that in order for a society to be able to exist the following basic social activities will have to be present and function well:

1. Protecting and conserving human and natural resources and property
2. Producing, exchanging, distributing, and consuming food, clothing, shelter, and other consumer goods and services
3. Transporting people and goods
4. Communicating ideas and feelings
5. Providing education
6. Providing recreation
7. Organizing and governing
8. Creating tools, techniques, and social arrangements
9. Expressing and satisfying aesthetic and spiritual impulses.[9]

Dr. Hanna goes on to claim that these activities "make up the totality of the citizenship activities," and anyone who is competent in them functions effectively in the society and is, therefore, a good citizen.

It appears that these basic social activities provide a meaningful scope for the social studies program, but just a listing of the activities does not give all the direction a teacher needs. For instance, it is not enough to advise a teacher that she should teach about organizing and governing. An area such as this is broad and complex and only the basic elements of it should be taught in the elementary school. So it is with all other social activities. Who defines these elements? Since the

---

[9] Paul R. Hanna and John R. Lee, "Generalizations from the Social Sciences," in: John U. Michaelis, ed., *Social Studies in Elementary Schools* (Washington, D. C.: National Council for the Social Studies, 1962), p. 69.

teachers are not specialists in all these areas it is obvious that they cannot perform this task alone.

Realizing this, Dr. Hanna took his approach a step further. With the help of specialists from each area he was able to identify the elements of each area in the form of basic generalizations. This was a significant step forward because teachers can now utilize these generalizations as the backbone of their program around which they can develop learning activities.

Plans are reported under way to carry this specific approach of social studies curriculum development an additional step forward. The identified generalizations which are stated in the language of the specialists, will be restructured and restated in terms of their more specific meaning for each of the eleven so-called expanding communities of men. According to Hanna these communities comprise the present sequence of the social studies program and they are the family, the school, the neighborhood, the community, the state, the region-of-states, the nation, the Americas, the western world, the Pacific, the world. With the completion of this phase of the project, the Hanna approach will have something concrete to offer to the individual teachers and the curriculum committees at the local level. Generally speaking, it is an approach which inspires confidence in the teachers because it does not require a complete departure from the present curriculum.

The American Council of Learned Societies and Educational Services Incorporated (ACLS-ESI) Project. The ultimate goal in this project is to develop a coherent, thoroughly integrated K–12 program based on the humanities and the social sciences. This program "would be sequential in its offerings, interdisciplinary in nature, and inductive in its method of approach to the disciplines."[10] Its sequence would be determined through the adoption of a chronological approach. The framework of this program would require it "to begin with man as he first emerged into a distinctive member of the primate family and to advance with him as he continued to develop a unique form of life encompassing the ability to symbolize and to create a complex society."[11] The specific

---

[10] Gordon B. Turner, "The American Council of Learned Societies and Curriculum Revision," in: Robert W. Heath, ed., *New Curricula* (New York: Harper and Row, Publishers), p. 147. More information and materials can be obtained from Educational Services Incorporated, 44–A Brattle St., Cambridge, Mass.

[11] *Ibid.* p. 148.

studies prescribed for the elementary grades include "man's origins and the history of Western man up through Minoan Crete and Mycenean Greece."[12]

The ACLS-ESI proposed program for the elementary grades has been criticized mainly because it ignores the present social context and "relies heavily on the children's being able and inclined themselves to apply what they learn to the world in which they live."[13]

The Harvard-Lexington Project. This project is an attempt to combine the advantages of the chronological, expanding communities, and problem approaches to social studies. The units suggested to be taught in each grade do not differ substantially from the units included in a conventional social studies program. The home and neighborhood are still being taught in the first grade. Greece and Rome are taught in the sixth grade. All units, however, are tied together by being oriented towards certain generalizations and a general theme assigned to each grade. The themes for K-6 are as follows:

K. The ways of man are more flexible and inventive than the ways of other animals.

1. Men have many different ways of meeting similar needs.

2. Human groups and institutions involve various patterns of norms, interactions and feelings.

3. Primitive societies have adapted to a variety of natural habitats.

4. Man finds new ways to control his relationship to his environment.

5. The industrial revolution has changed the production and distribution of goods and services and has created new opportunities and problems for human society.

6. Man's acts of inquiry, creativity, and expression evolve from and influence his total way of life.[14]

United States Office of Education Project Social Studies. The Cooperative Research Branch of the Department of Health, Education, and Welfare has initiated twelve curriculum projects in social studies all together known as Project Social Studies. Some of them are limited to

---

[12] *Ibid.*, p. 153.

[13] Joseph C. Grannis, "The Framework of the Social Studies Curriculum," *The National Elementary Principal*, Vol. XLII (April 1963), p. 24.

[14] *Ibid.*, p. 25.

one course in one discipline while others propose to develop entire curricula. The majority of them are oriented towards the secondary school. Those concerned with the development of entire curricula K–12 or K–14 are being briefly reviewed in this section. There are only two of them. Since both are still in development stages, teachers are urged to contact the institutions in which the projects take place and ask for reports on further developments and for related materials. The institutions and the names of the project directors are given below.

One of these projects aims to develop an "articulated curriculum" for grades K–14 and is directed by Edith West at the University of Minnesota. In the first progress report published, Dr. West writes that her staff believed "the prime purpose of the social studies curriculum should be to develop citizens capable of coping with problems in the modern age."[15] In order to arrive at a curriculum which would contribute to the realization of this objective, the social scientists were consulted first. After they gave the conceptual framework of their own particular disciplines, they were asked to identify "the key concepts which cut across the disciplines." As Dr. West pointed out "the concept of culture becomes the unifying concept for the entire curriculum."[16] She goes on to say that the comparative approach plays a very important role in this curriculum. Values and the development of the thinking process, are not to be neglected.

Concerning the elementary level Dr. West says, "At the present time, the staff envisions heavy emphasis upon concepts from anthropology, sociology, and geography in the primary grades, with the addition of many economic concepts in grade 4. Although they have rejected the typical expanding horizons organization, they have selected topics which are close to the life of pupils and have provided a comparative study of these topics in selected places throughout the world."[17] The family, for example, would be one such topic. For the upper grades in the elementary school the Minnesota project proposes a greater emphasis upon geography and history as separate disciplines.

---

[15] Edith West, "University of Minnesota—An Articulated Curriculum for Grades K–14," *Social Education*, Vol. 29 (April 1965), p. 209. More information can be obtained from Dr. West, College of Education, University of Minnesota, Minneapolis, Minn.

[16] *Ibid.*

[17] *Ibid.* p. 210.

Dr. Roy A. Price of Syracuse University is directing a similar project. The specific objectives of this project were stated by the director as follows: "(1) To identify the major concepts from the social sciences and allied disciplines that appear to be appropriate for an elementary and secondary program in the social studies; (2) to examine the major workways of these disciplines . . .; and (3) to develop and evaluate at three grade levels illustrative materials for use by teachers and students that effectively translate the concepts and workways into classroom practice."[18]

Work on the first and second objectives above has been completed. In a publication entitled *Major Concepts for Social Studies*[19] substantive concepts, value concepts, and concepts of method are identified. The substantive concepts include: sovereignty of nation, conflict, the industrialization-urbanization syndrome, secularization, compromise and adjustment, comparative advantage, power, morality and choice, input and output, scarcity, saving, the modified market economy, habitat and its significance, culture, institution, social control, social change, and interaction. The value concepts include: dignity of man, empathy, government by consent of the governed, loyalty, and freedom and equality. Included among the concepts of method are: historical method and point of view, the geographical approach, and causation. Under the concepts of method the following techniques and aspects of method have also been identified: observation, classification and measurement, analysis and synthesis, questions and answers, objectivity, skepticism, interpretation, evaluation, and evidence.

Presently the staff is working in the production of materials related to the third objective of the project.

The Elkhart, Indiana Experiment in Economic Education. Professor Lawrence Senesh experimented with methods and materials in the teaching of the basic structure of the discipline of Economics to primary grade children beginning with the first grade. This project is now developing into a complete K–12 social studies program in which all social science disciplines are utilized. It appears that the

---

[18] Roy A. Price, "Syracuse University—Social Science Concepts and Workways as the Basis for Curriculum Revision," *Social Education*, Volume 29 (April 1965), p. 218.

[19] This publication is available from the Social Studies Curriculum Center, 409 Maxwell Hall, Syracuse University, Syracuse, New York 13210; price $1.50.

Senesh program is following from grade to grade Paul Hanna's expanding horizons approach. The treatment of each setting, however, is more intellectual and reality oriented than it has been in the past.

The program being developed by Dr. Senesh and made commercially available by Science Research Associates, is built around a number of basic characteristics. As he wrote, it is social reality oriented, problem oriented, structured, interdisciplinary, K–12 oriented, time and space oriented, and future oriented.[20]

The Contra Costa County Program. This program was developed by the late Hilda Taba and is described in one of her publications as "a system of thinking about and planning a curriculum."[21] Taba stresses the importance of generalizations which serve as the elements around which appropriate content can be placed.

The teaching strategies suggested by Taba involve three cognitive tasks, as she calls them. The first task is concept formation. "Concepts are formed as students respond to questions which require them: (1) to enumerate items; (2) to find a basis for grouping items that are familiar in some respect; (3) to identify the common characteristics of items in a group; (4) to label the groups; and (5) to subsume items that they have enumerated under those labels."[22] The second cognitive task consists of interpreting, inferring, and generalizing. Finally, the third cognitive task is the application of known principles and facts to explain unfamiliar phenomena or predict consequences from familiar and known conditions.

Other programs reflecting the new trends in social studies education include the Anthropology Curriculum Project at the University of Georgia, the Greater Cleveland Social Science Program and others less well known.

What can the teachers do?

As was pointed out earlier in this chapter, none of the projects described above promises a standard national curriculum which will eliminate all the weaknesses in the social studies program. In the words

---

[20] Lawrence Senesh, "The Pattern of the Economic Curriculum," *Social Education*, Volume 32 (January 1968), pp. 47–50, 59.

[21] Hilda Taba, *Teachers' Handbook for Elementary Social Studies* (Palo Alto: Addison-Wesley Publishing Company, Inc., 1967), p. viii.

[22] *Ibid.*, p. 92.

of Donald W. Robinson, "The greatest promise for improved instruction comes not from carefully organized national efforts to reconstruct a curriculum, but from attention to promoting imaginative teaching and an academic excitement that succeeds almost regardless of the curriculum."[23] Although a sound system of guidelines is essential to the improvement of teaching social studies, the greatest hope for remedying the situation rests with the teachers at the local level. What can they do?

Provide for a sound structure. The first thing to do is to give a new substance to the structure of the program. So far it has been dominated by randomly selected activities. The value of these activities has never been systematically determined in terms of their contributions to significant social learnings. There is a need for screening the activities and structuring them around basic learnings or generalizations. Teachers will be able to do this with the rather indirect assistance of social scientists in a manner which is described in the following paragraphs.

State Departments of Education and local school systems usually develop their own social studies courses. In the majority of cases, however, what these courses consist of is a number of topics and activities. What is usually missing are basic generalizations from the social sciences which can make these topics and activities meaningful. Unless the generalizations become the substance of the program and the topics and activities the means through which to grasp these generalizations, the program will lack a sound structure.

Social scientists have been very reluctant in the past in supplying the teachers with the much needed generalizations. It is only very recently, and mainly through the stimulation provided by the projects described earlier in this chapter, that they have assumed an active role in the improvement of the public school social studies curricula. Special publications written by social scientists which contain basic generalizations from all social sciences are now available for the use of the teachers. One such publication, *The Social Sciences: Foundations of the Social Studies*, edited by John U. Michaelis and A. Montgomery Johnston was made available by Allyn and Bacon, Inc. in 1965.

The University of Indiana recently sponsored a series of seminars

---

[23] Donald W. Robinson, "Ferment in the Social Studies," *Social Education*, Vol. 27 (November 1963), p. 362.

on the various social sciences. The purpose of these seminars was to bring together well-known social scientists who would present scholarly viewpoints on geography, political science, history, sociology, economics, and anthropology—identifying basic generalizations in each of the disciplines mentioned. Furthermore, professional educators were responsible for translating the identified social science generalizations into meaningful learning experiences for elementary and secondary school students. The outcomes of the seminars were published by Charles E. Merrill Books, Inc., in 1965 in the following volumes:

The Study of Anthropology by Pertti J. Pelto
Political Science: An Informal Overview by Francis T. Sorauf
Geography: Its Scope and Spirit by Jan O. M. Broek
Sociology: The Study of Man in Society by Caroline B. Rose
The Nature and the Study of History by Henry Steele Commager
Economics and Its Significance by Richard S. Martin and Reuden
    G. Miller

Besides the authors, there were other consultants involved. Raymond H. Muessig and Vincent R. Rogers, both professional educators, were the editors of the series and wrote the last chapters containing suggested methods for teachers.

With the state or local courses of study on one hand, and with these or similar sources of generalizations on the other, each teacher can design a soundly structured curriculum for herself. To achieve this, teachers should match the suggested topics for their grades with related generalizations. These generalizations will, then, become the focus of their teaching and the substance of their program.

In an institute which was sponsored by the State of New York and directed by this writer, the participating teachers worked out a matching between the topics suggested in the recently revised state syllabus and the generalizations listed in the Michaelis and Johnston book which was mentioned earlier. Examples of this from each grade are shown below:

Grade	*Topic*	*Generalization*
Kinder-garten	Economic organization—Family jobs and responsibilities—division of	Cooperation is illustrated by the way in which members of families and other more inti-

labor.

mately related social groups tend to work together in performing functions of community living and in attaining common goals. (p. 337)

First   Political organization— Introduction to the idea of democracy—the president and his election.

Democracy implies a way of life as well as a form of government. (p. 317)

Second   Social Organization— Other community organizations such as service clubs.

The work of society is performed through organized groups. Groups differ because of their purposes, their institutions, heritage, and location. (p. 333)

Third   Northern Forest or Taiga community—typical climatic conditions.

Major climatic regions coincide approximately with major vegetative zones because vegetation is related to climatic conditions. (p. 309)

Fourth   Leaders

The behavior of individuals is related to the structure and organization of the group in which they are placed. Differences also furnish a basis for flexibility and creativity, which are essential to social change and development. (p. 332)

Fifth   The United States— Introduction to governmental system (Federal)

Government cannot be effective unless it has the flexibility to cope with new conditions. The constitution of the United States provides for the flexibility to meet changing conditions. (p. 317)

Sixth   The Middle East— Historical

Change has been a universal condition of human society. Change and progress are, however, not necessarily synonymous. Many civilizations have risen and fallen. (p. 313)

An approach such as the one just suggested implies that the teachers have an understanding of the generalizations. Unless the teachers have a clear and thorough understanding of them, they will not be able to develop the generalizations into words and situations that the child can understand. Knowing that the general education of elementary teachers is not as adequate as it should be, this cannot be assumed or expected. Teachers are urged, therefore, to take as many courses as they can in the subject matter areas along with the necessary methods courses.

Eliminate trivial content and repetition. With the selection of generalizations the teacher establishes central goals for the study of various topics. Generalizations, of course, represent relationships of broad applicability and they are usually written in the language of specialists: in this case, social scientists. They have to be translated into the vocabulary of elementary school children and illustrated with appropriate situations demonstrating the relationships. Teachers are cautioned to make sure that the essence of the generalization is not lost in the effort. Social studies will otherwise end where it was, involving youngsters in activities without purpose. When there is no purpose, there is no way of knowing if an activity is trivial or important.

Besides the lack of generalizations, there is another factor mainly responsible for repetitious content. This is the "expanding environment" approach used for many years in the selection and placement of social studies content.

When psychologists expounded the idea that children learn best when dealing with their immediate environment, curriculum specialists imposed geographic boundaries for each grade's studies. All learning activities had to be selected from within these specified boundaries. The domain of the first grade came to be the home and the school; the second grade was to limit itself to the neighborhood; the third grade dealt with the local community; the fourth grade could study the local state; the fifth grade children were found capable of expanding to the United States and the Western Hemisphere; the sixth grade children were to cover the rest of the world.

Theoretically this approach appears sound, but it allows too much emphasis on the "here and now" of the child. The result of this overemphasis is repetition and lack of challenge especially in the beginning grades. This in turn results in loss of interest in learning. Children come to school with high expectations. They come to school to face new and challenging things. They become disappointed when they run into an over-simplified curriculum.

To eliminate unnecessary repetition, this writer proposed a modification of the "expanding environment" approach.[24] The elements of this modified approach are not entirely new. However, they suggest a systematic strategy to be used in the selection of learning activities. Two parts in the child's environment should be recognized. One is that which the child explores before he comes to school together with what he is capable of exploring by himself while in school. The other is that in which the child needs the help of the school. The schools should carefully draw the lines between these two parts of the child's environment and avoid being concerned with the first one except for purposes of motivation. The principle of the "expanding environment" modified as suggested here would look in a diagrammatical form as shown in Figure 1.

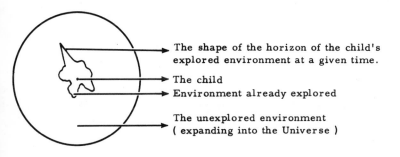

The shape of the horizon of the child's explored environment at a given time.

The child

Environment already explored

The unexplored environment (expanding into the Universe)

Figure 1

The child is in the center. Around him is his immediate environment which he explored to some extent before entering the elementary school. The irregular line enclosing the child marks the boundaries of the child's already explored environment. The irregularity of the line

---

[24] Theodore Kaltsounis, "A Modification of the 'Expanding Environment' Approach," *The Social Studies*, Volume 35 (March 1964), pp. 99–102.

shows that the child has advanced more in his explorations in some areas while he is behind in others. This is due mostly to the special interests which the children have developed. It should be emphasized that the distance of the boundaries between the explored and unexplored environments is different from child to child. Also, the irregularities of the boundaries are different from child to child. These kinds of differences, determined on an average basis, would also be present from group to group or from grade to grade.

If a teacher is to do an effective job, he has first to find the distance of the boundaries and determine their irregularities, and then proceed from there. In other words, what is demanded here is an intensive diagnostic procedure which will provide a social studies curriculum not of what is close to the child in terms of the familiar, but of the unknown that is close to the child in terms of its association with the familiar. A program designed in this way will be challenging and at the same time will take into consideration the past experiences of the youngsters.

It appears that a trend toward a modified form of the "expanding environment" approach is becoming popular. Many of the more recent courses of study suggest departure from the original notion. While they retain the topics suggested by the "expanding environment" approach, they go beyond the traditional boundaries in order to compare situations and, in so doing, to strengthen various generalizations. The primary grades child, for instance, is no longer limited to his own community. He is given many opportunities to compare life in his community with community life in other parts of the world. In this day and age this is not difficult at all.

Summary

The first step in an effort to improve the curriculum is to know what is wrong with it. Unless those concerned are alarmed by the deficiencies of the present social studies curriculum, there will probably not be strong motivation to change.

The present curriculum is expository and not built around generalizations. Evidence reveals that it is not as up-to-date as the interests of the children in today's world. In many cases the curriculum is outdated or gives the wrong picture of modern society. In the primary grades the curriculum is too easy while in the upper grades there is too much "covering" of content. There is a need for a sound structure.

Several projects across the nation attempt to give structure to the program through the use of generalizations from the social sciences. Even though these projects will not be nearly the entire solution, teachers can benefit from them. They can apply the generalizations which are defined by specialists in order to provide central aims for their programs. With these generalizations in mind and by modifying the "expanding environment" approach, the teachers will be able to select challenging and meaningful learning activities for the children in the elementary school.

Building a Strong Program for
the Primary Grades

3

Building a Strong Program for the Primary Grades

One of the major social studies trends is the conscious effort on the part of curriculum workers and teachers to base new programs on the nature of the learner and the learning process as revealed and defined by recent and contemporary researchers.

The nature of the learner—his interests, his experiential background, and his capability to grasp abstract ideas—has always been a basic consideration in curriculum development. In regard to social studies in the primary grades, however, this factor is of more importance now than ever before due to the fact that the new direction suggested for the primary grades' social studies program is dictated by the changes in the nature of the children. It is only logical, then, that in order for curriculum workers and teachers to understand and accept the reasoning underlying the new programs, they must become familiar with these changes in the children's nature.

Also, teachers should study the latest developments in learning theory, particularly as it applies to the primary grades. The conceptualization approach appears to be most promising in eliminating trivial content and bridging the gap between the elementary knowledge offered in the primary grades and the more advanced knowledge offered in the upper grades. The most outstanding and articulate spokesman for the conceptualization approach is Jerome Bruner.

Obviously, the changes which have taken place in the nature of children and the implications of conceptualization for the primary grades constitute the most important underlying factors for a sound curriculum in these grades.

Strengthening of the program could be achieved without abandoning the present framework of community studies. Inherent in this suggested method, however, is the recommendation that the community should not be regarded as a geographic entity isolated from the rest of the world. Its interdependence with the rest of the world should be studied and adequate avenues should be provided to take the children wherever their interest, imagination and curiosity lead them. In the light of this approach some of the present units taught will have to be eliminated or at least given a different direction. An example of this is the overemphasis on Indian life.

The recommendations introduced thus far, make it possible for a more substantive content. But the changes in the primary grades' social studies program are not, and should not, be limited to the content needed to achieve objectives of a cognitive nature alone. Social studies skills previously reserved for third grade and above have been integrated into kindergarten, first and second grade studies as well. An effort is being made in this chapter to assure the teacher that this is a move in the right direction, because it places the teaching of social studies within the proper context.

This chapter is concluded with brief descriptions of structured programs already implemented in the primary grades. This was thought to be the most practical and convincing way of suggesting that the recommendations made in this chapter are not merely theorizing.

Underlying factors

There are many underlying factors which influence and determine the social studies curriculum of the elementary school. No effort will be made to present them all in this chapter because teachers are usually familiar with them. The factors presented have been selected because their nature has changed and, as a result, they appear to be the primary causes for the obsolescence of existing social studies curriculum, especially in the primary grades.

Children's interests should not be the main determinants of the curriculum. Nevertheless, they constitute a very important factor in deciding what should be taught. In the past the "here and now" was stressed because it was felt that the children's interests were associated primarily with their everyday experiences. It was because of this that the primary grades' curriculum was limited to the boundaries of the local community.

The association of interests with everyday experiences is a psychological principle which still holds true. It should not be neglected in the planning of learning experiences. The curriculum, however, which this principle originally dictated ought to be changed because the children's interests are no longer what they used to be years ago.

The media of mass communication and the rapid developments in the field of transportation have expanded the immediate environment of children. Many places which are far geographically, have become, in a psychological sense, parts of the immediate environment of the children.

John D. McAulay[1] reported in 1962 on a study in which he found that children's interests definitely go beyond the immediate community. As a matter of fact first graders indicated great interest in the study of geographic environments different from their own such as the desert, the jungle, lands of the elephant, and the country of the reindeer. Probably influenced by television, they wanted to study about the pioneer days of the past and about the days of the gladiators. They expressed concern about such things as the sleeping habits of other people, the toys and games of children in other countries, and the housing of other lands.

Children enrolled in the second grade were interested about Africa, Japan, and the North Pole. They wanted to know why we

[1] John D. McAulay, "Social Studies Interests of the Primary Grades Child," *Social Education*, Vol. 26 (April 1962), pp. 138–145.

have a President and a Statue of Liberty. Second graders expressed awareness of social differences between groups and nations and wanted to know more about these differences.

Third graders showed interest in geographic concepts encompassing the whole world. They raised questions related to the economic relationships of the United States and Africa, and to the lack of food in India. The third graders' historical interests concerned the beginnings of settlements as well as the beginnings of various institutions. Also, they wondered about the relationship of various events in American History. The interest in social differences between groups and nations, which was shown by the second graders, was even stronger with the third graders. They were interested in the differences between the United States and the Soviet Union, between the negro and the white segments of American society, and in some degree they were concerned about the differences between the more developed and less developed nations of the world.

It is evident from McAulay's study that the interests of the children in the primary grades, upon which the existing social studies program was supposedly based, are no longer confined to the milkman, the fireman and the corner policeman. This expansion of interests caused the children to be ahead of the present program. Several studies have been published in the last few years which focus attention on this change. This writer[2] examined third graders to determine the extent to which they knew the third grade social studies cognitive content prior to instruction. On the average children knew approximately 37 percent of the content appearing in third grade textbooks of nation-wide use. There were several children who knew nearly everything they were supposed to study during the following eight or nine months.

Ralph Preston[3] cites a study by Betty Lowry in which she tested and interviewed second grade children on concepts they were about to study. Her findings indicated that the children on the average knew from 64 to 85 percent of the concepts.

---

[2] Theodore Kaltsounis, "A Study Concerning Third Graders' Knowledge of Social Studies Content Prior to Instruction," *The Journal of Educational Research*, Vol. 57 (March 1964), pp. 345–349.

[3] Ralph C. Preston, "What Social Studies Content for Primary Grades?", *Social Education*, Vol. 29 (March 1965), p. 147.

A study of first-graders by Charlotte Huck led her to conclude, "Teachers must recognize the vast amount of knowledge possessed by a six-year old at the beginning of his academic education and utilize these learnings resulting from exposure to many sources instead of decrying them"[4]

Another underlying factor which had a tremendous impact upon the elementary school social studies program is found in Jerome Bruner's ideas about teaching and learning. Bruner bases his ideas upon the central concept of the structure of knowledge. He claims that knowledge is interrelated in terms of basic principles and that understanding of these basic principles makes knowledge more meaningful. Bruner goes on to claim that awareness of the inter-relatedness of knowledge contributes to much greater retention. On the other hand, understanding of basic principles makes "transfer of training" much more effective.

The idea with which Bruner had his greatest impact on the curriculum of the primary grades has to do with the readiness for learning as related to the structure of knowledge. As he pointed out in his book, *The Process of Education*,[5] the basic principles of any subject may be taught to anybody at any age level in some intellectually honest form. In other words, Bruner suggests that the foundations of any subject can be taught in some form at the primary grades. He implies that teachers should not waste the school time of children with bits of descriptive information presented in an isolated form when they could deal with basic concepts and fundamental principles.

The process of conceptualization, about which there has been so much talk recently, and the majority of the projects for curriculum revision which were described in the previous chapter, have been inspired by Bruner. Reports in *Social Education* and other journals indicate that numerous school systems and individual teachers have put into practice Bruner's ideas by successfully teaching fundamental social science principles to the children in the primary grades. Teachers and administrators are urged to study Bruner's writings, not just

---

[4] Charlotte Huck, "Children Learn from their Culture," *Educational Leadership*, Vol. 13 (December 1955), pp. 171–175.

[5] Jerome S. Bruner, *The Process of Education* (New York: Vintage Books, 1960), pp. 33–54.

reports dealing with the application of his ideas. Some of these reports are reviewed near the end of this chapter.

Other factors to be considered are the various limitations of young children. The attitudes and values of children in this age group are not yet settled and their judgment of what they experience is easier to sway than in later years. Children in the primary grades have a language handicap, especially in reading. Furthermore, six-, seven-, and eight-year olds are under greater parental influence. It is likely that the school has not yet become the trustworthy authority on values.

Providing for structure through the use of generalizations from social sciences

In spite of all criticism directed against the social studies program of the primary grades, the study of the local community should remain the principal focus for the first, second, and third grades. The local community is neither a single nor a simple topic for study because within its setting and operation all basic social functions can be identified for study. Basic principles of sociology, history, anthropology, political science, geography, and economics can be taught through the local community.

Besides, it is psychologically important for the teachers to retain community studies as the main emphasis, because it is easier for the the majority of them to orient themselves to a new approach in the study of the community rather than to ask them to teach something entirely different. A completely new curriculum will make the teachers feel a pressure for re-education, and all their files and resources accumulated over the years will be useless. Sizable amounts of money would have to be spent to restock the school libraries.

It is not desirable to replace community studies, but to reorganize and structure them to teach those elements which will contribute most towards the development and understanding of basic social concepts and generalizations.

On the basis of the guidelines given in the previous chapter, the first step toward providing structure in the primary grades' social studies program is to single out a number of generalizations which are related to the nature and operations of the community. Any one of the published sources, which have already been mentioned, or others which will be published in the future, could be used. Make sure the generalizations are stated by social scientists or, at least, that they meet with their approval.

It should be pointed out at this point that the various sources list a number of generalizations from each discipline in the social sciences. Of course, not all of them could or should be taught to young children. Each teacher or committee of teachers should select those generalizations from each area which they think most important. They should also select as individuals those which they understand best.

Usually sources of generalizations such as the ones suggested in this book make sure to list those which are basic and accepted by the majority of the social scientists. However, a variation from one list to another is obvious. It is the flux and changing nature of the content of social sciences which allows this and it should not be disturbing. As a matter of fact, this should be a source of comfort for a grade teacher when she discovers that she did not choose for her grade the same generalizations which a teacher of a similar grade has chosen.

Below are some of the generalizations that can be integrated into the local community studies in the primary grades. They were selected by the author from Michaelis and Johnston's book, *The Social Sciences— Foundations of the Social Studies*. The discipline which each reflects is indicated in parentheses.

1. Productive resources are scarce, and human wants are unlimited. Since man cannot satisfy all of his desires for material goods, he must make choices. (Economics)
2. Life on the earth is influenced by the earth's (global) shape, its size, and its set of motions. (Geography)
3. Soils are altered by nature and man. Nature combines the action of climate, vegetation, and animals on parent materials to produce regional variations in soils. (Geography)
4. Man constantly seeks to satisfy his needs for food, clothing and shelter and his other wants; in so doing, he attempts to adapt, shape, utilize, and exploit the earth. (Geography)
5. Change has been a universal condition of human society. (History)

6. Interdependence has been a constant and important factor in human relationships everywhere. (History)
7. Although certain historical customs and institutions have characterized individual civilizations or nations in the past, men in every age and place have made use of basic social functions in adjusting themselves to their world. (History)
8. In a democracy, geovernment is the servant of the people; people are not the servants of government. Government is by right an institution made by man for man. The source of authority resides in the people. (Political Science)
9. The citizen has civic responsibility as well as rights. (Political Science)
10. A democratic society depends on citizens who are intellectually and morally fit to conduct their government. (Political Science)
11. The culture under which a person matures exerts a powerful influence on him throughout his life. (Anthropology)
12. Human beings, regardless of their social or ethnic background, are nearly all capable of participating in making contributions to any culture. (Anthropology)
13. The work of society is performed through organized groups. Group membership requires that individuals undertake varied roles involving differing responsibilities, rights and opportunities. (Sociology)
14. Communication is basic to the existence of culture and groups. (Sociology)
15. National migration develops cultural diversity within a group and cultural diffusion among groups. (Sociology)[6]

It should be emphasized that this is neither an absolute nor a complete list of generalizations for the primary grades. Others could be added or used as substitutes. Depending on the conditions of a class some teachers may use a much shorter list.

The next step in the development of a structured curriculum is to take each one of the selected generalizations and determine specific objectives in terms of children's behaviors. These objectives should be of the cognitive as well as the affective type. In other words, they

---

[6] John U. Michaelis and A. Montgomery Johnston, ed., *The Social Sciences— Foundations of the Social Studies* (Boston: Allyn and Bacon, Inc., 1965), pp. 306–339.

should be oriented towards the understanding of concepts and relationships as well as towards the development of certain attitudes, dispositions and commitments. Following the determination of specific behavioral objectives, or concurrently, the teacher should be thinking about and developing the learning experiences which will enable the children to reach the objectives.

In order to illustrate this step, the last generalization from the above list will be utilized. This generalization reads as follows: "National migration develops cultural diversity within a group and cultural diffusion among groups." A young kindergarten teacher directed the attention of her children towards identifying those children in the class who have come from other communities in various parts of the country. Some of the new children were aware of the reasons which caused their families to move. The teacher, then, created some hypothetical reasons which could force the families of some of the children to leave their present community. She suggested, for instance, that the local aluminum plant might close down or that some of the fathers might be offered a better job in some other part of the country.

A second grade was faced with the problem of raising some money to buy an aquarium. They had tried several ways to do this but they still needed money. The teacher asked the new children if they, in the school previously attended, had used any other ways to raise money. Some new ways were then suggested. This experience was used by the teacher to have the children identify some of the ways of life and new skills that migrant people have brought into the community. This, in turn, led to a study of the variety of ways in which the basic social functions operate in different communities.

Another group of more sophisticated children looked into the history of the community to find instances in which the generalization could apply. It was discovered that a particular neighborhood was developed at the time a new plant was put into operation. They also discovered that with the expansion of the local university, new churches were established in the surrounding area to meet the religious needs of students and faculty who came from all over the country. Experiences of this kind also helped the children to see the application of the generalization in developments that have taken place in other communities and other countries.

Most of the activities described lead to the realization of cognitive objectives. Along with the understanding of the generalization, the teacher should strive to have the children accept the idea of migration, to make them less provincial and more tolerant of new people arriving in school or in the ommunity. While the cognitive objectives should dominate teaching, the teacher should always try to develop in children those commitments necessary to enable them to practice the democratic way of life.

Teaching community studies in its wider setting

Structure will put substance in the primary program without having to abandon the community studies. In selecting the learning experiences, however, the community should not be treated in isolation. To do so is unrealistic, because no community can exist and function today without links with the outside world. Further, it means ignoring the children's interests which extend far beyond local boundaries.

Paul Hanna suggested that in order for a society to be able to function well, certain social functions, such as government, transportation, and communication must exist. These functions are present and can be studied at the community level. All of them, however, expand and are connected with the surrounding communities, the state, the nation, and in many cases the world. The community, therefore, should be studied in its wider setting.

Teaching about the grocery store has been a long time practice for primary grade teachers. The teaching of this topic has been criticized in the last few years because it was taught in a superficial manner. The children would spend a considerable amount of time building a grocery store in some corner of the classroom and studying the arrangement of the various food items by using empty cans and boxes. Also, the children would go through the process of shopping and paying with make-believe money for what was purchased. Schools and teachers have been criticized because this approach does not help the children learn much that they do not already know.

If the children are to learn something basic which will better enable them to get to know the community and its relationship to the outside world, the study of the grocery store should be approached from the point of view of the production and the distribution of food. Here are some basic questions to be asked: What made possible the supermarkets and caused the corner grocery stores to start disappearing? What are some of the advantages of the supermarkets? What difference did refrigeration make as far as the kinds of foods available through the years? From what places does food come? How is it transported? Is there any relationship between the supermarkets and the federal government?

Some of these questions are basic economic questions and they can be dealt with to a great extent at the primary level. Take for example the last question, which may appear to be the most difficult one. A teacher taught it through activities such as the following: Cans of various foods were brought to class and the children were asked to identify the kind of food in each by referring to the labels. The children's reliance on the labels was shaken by switching the labels prior to opening the cans in their presence. To lead the children to the role of the federal government in this case, the following question was asked: Who makes sure that manufacturers put in the cans whatever they indicate on the labels?

When community studies are structured through the use of generalizations and the various topics are taught as suggested in the previous illustration, the children deal with the outside world without abandoning the community as the central focus of attention. On the other hand this approach brings the program in harmony with children's interests without disorienting the teachers completely.

Use the comparative approach

Tracing the connections of community life to the outside world is one approach to enrich the present primary social studies program. Another approach, which has gained wide acceptance in the recent years, is the comparative approach. At the present time in most schools the comparative approach is being used at the third-grade level. What this approach entails is comparing or contrasting the local community life with that in communities in other parts of the country or world.

It is recommended that Hanna's basic social functions serve as the basis for the comparison. These functions were treated at some length in the previous chapter and they are: conservation, production and distribution, transportation, communication, education, recreation, government, technology, expression and satisfaction of aesthetic and spiritual impulses.

Also, it is recommended that those communities should be selected which represent parts of the country with a different type of community life. When looking for communities outside the United States, a world-wide representation should again be a basic criterion. Communities from each continent should be selected on the basis of what could best motivate the children. It could be that the ancestors of many of the children in a particular class come from a specific country. It could be that relatives of certain children have recently visited a particular country. Perhaps some countries appear very often in the news or the United States is involved in the affairs of a nation as we have been involved in Korea, the Congo, Viet Nam and elsewhere.

Something should be said here about the study of the life of Indians. It used to be that the Indians constituted one of the most favorable units for the primary grades. For some teachers this continues to be true even today. There is considerable controversy, however, as to the relative value of the study of the Indians. In view of this controversy the teachers face a decision.

At a meeting of the New York State Council for the Social Studies one elementary school teacher questioned a publisher on the obvious de-emphasis of Indian life in the textbooks. His reply was in the form of a question paraphrased as follows: Is there anything significant which we inherited from the Indians? A noted political scientist delivered a lecture recently on "Education for the New Politics" in which he expressed concern because his little girl was devoting a great part of her homework tracing Indian trails. He did not mind the Indian trails, but he would have preferred that they be those leading to New Delhi.

Primitive community life is exemplified through the study of American Indians, but it is also exemplified by life in parts of Africa or Australia. The Indians are a part of American history, but to what extent they should be treated in public schools is something which each teacher will have to decide in view of everything else which should be taught. The trend appears to be less emphasis on Indians than in previous years, at least less emphasis on the Indians of the past.

The development of skills in primary grades

As mentioned in the first chapter, there are two types of skills which should concern teachers in social studies. On the one hand there are those skills considered important in the every day person to person, person to group, and group to group relationships. On the other hand there are a number of study skills and techniques peculiar to the social studies and the process of inquiry. Skills such as cooperation, tolerance and respecting each other's right to speak, belong in the first category. The second category includes skills such as map making and reading, interpretation of graphs, distinguishing between reporting and propaganda, problem solving and others.

It should always be kept in mind that skills are means to some end. Unless this is completely understood and accepted there can be no realistic approach to the development of social studies skills. If skills are to mean something in the lives of children, they should be developed in a natural way. Cooperation cannot be developed by setting aside a 20 minute period a week. It can only be developed when the teacher sees to it that all class affairs are conducted in the spirit of cooperation. Problem solving skills can best be developed through the involvement of children in problem situations related to the content. As a matter of fact, all content should be converted into problems for which the children should seek answers under the direction of the teacher.

While the development of skills is a vital part of the social studies program in terms of objectives, skills themselves do not constitute any part of the substance of the social studies content. The substance of the content is cognitive in nature. Skills are partly ways of dealing with this content and partly a way of life within the framework of the classroom and school. The implication of this view is that the objectives of a lesson plan cannot be skills alone. Objectives in the nature of skills should always appear in the form of riders to cognitive objectives.

In the past a serious mistake was made in the determination of the primary grades' social studies curriculum. Skills became the only objectives of the curriculum and social studies deteriorated to a "subject" of good manners. Very few, if any, substantive social studies objectives in the form of concepts and generalizations were involved.

Maps, graphs and charts. In the past, maps, charts and graphs were not usually introduced before the third grade. Now there is a trend to introduce them as early as kindergarten. The children are now directed to make maps of their classroom, school, neighborhood and community. They learn how to use symbols for various landmarks and how to relate these landmarks and determine direction. All these activities in the study of the community prove most helpful in enabling the youngsters to learn later how to read and interpret the various types of commercial maps.

Simple activities can also be used to introduce the meaning and function of graphs and charts. A two column graph, for example, can be made to show the children who were born in the community and those who came from other communities. A chart can be made to show the school enrollment or the population of the community in the last ten years. Again, it is emphasized that skills should be taught in connection with intended cognitive learnings and not in isolation.

Implemented programs

Obviously, the trend is toward a structured program for the primary grades which would be based on the social sciences. This trend, however, has become a source of apprehension for many teachers, because they cannot see themselves teaching Sociology or Anthropology to the primary grade children. This chapter was written with the conviction that it can be done. But to further illustrate the point, certain programs which have already been implemented along the lines suggested in this chapter are briefly being brought to the attention of the teachers. For more details the reader may refer to the original sources as footnoted.

Bernard Spodek[7] reported in *Social Education* a successful program with kindergarten children. He set up an experimental situation with the goal to determine the extent to which children at this level could grasp basic concepts in social sciences. The concepts selected were related to the topic "New York as a Harbor." The following statement could serve as an illustration of the concepts involved: "Changes that have taken place in the harbor can be understood in relation to changes

---

[7] Bernard Spodek, "Developing Social Science Concepts in Kindergarten," *Social Education*, Vol. 27 (May 1963), pp. 253–257.

in technology and changes in the needs of people." Relationships such as this were broken down into more specific understandings that kindergarten children could attain. The results led to the conclusion that kindergarten children are capable of starting to develop significant social science concepts.

Mary Rusnak,[8] disturbed by the simplicity of the first grade program, attempted to introduce such concepts as historical sequence, cause and effect, geographical space, and adaptation to environment. She also attempted to compare simple and complex societies. All work was done within the framework of a typical first-grade curriculum which included units in the home and the community. The results were favorable as far as acquisition of new knowledge and the development of more interest in social studies.

In 1959 the elementary supervisors of Bucks County schools in Pennsylvania started work to form a new social studies program for the primary grades based on generalizations from the social sciences.[9] The main topics of consideration were citizenship, geography and people of other lands. In 1961 the teachers were paid to participate in a workshop in which they studied the suggested program and put it in a final form. A few of the generalizations selected are listed below:

> United States citizenship is a privilege which carries with it rights and responsibilities.
> Using flat maps, one may study in detail more limited areas of the world.
> People live in groups.
> People use the resources of the earth to satisfy physical needs.
> People seek to express themselves physically, aesthetically, and spiritually.
> People need some form of government.

After one year of implementation the fifteen teachers involved evaluated the program and some of their findings indicated that primary children need to and can work with a great deal more social studies content than primary children of several years ago; that most primary children are interested in distant lands; that primary children of

---

[8] Mary Rusnak, "Introducing Social Studies in the First Grade," *Social Education*, Vol. 25 (October 1961), pp. 291–292.

[9] Gloria Cammarota, "New Emphasis in Social Studies for the Primary Grades," *Social Education*, Vol. 27 (February 1963), pp. 77–80.

all levels enjoy map work and have little difficulty understanding it; that there is a great wealth of films, filmstrips, and books written at primary reading levels—as well as maps and globes with which to teach the concepts and generalizations identified.

Also, investigations such as those by McAulay[10] and Rushdoony[11] demonstrate the ability of primary children to deal with maps.

SUMMARY

It became clear in the last several years that the social studies curriculum for the primary grades needed to be reorganized and brought up-to-date. There are several factors which necessitated this. Due to the rapid development of the mass media, the interests of primary children have been expanded. It was found that children are capable of learning more than previously assumed. Bruner has convinced the educational world that the structure of disciplines contributes to more and better learning even in the primary grades.

A sound and structured curriculum in social studies can be provided for the primary grades without abandoning the community studies as the main focus. From a list of generalizations made available by social scientists, teachers may select those which they can relate to community studies. Then, they can design learning activities which would assist the children to develop these generalizations.

The community ought to be studied not in isolation, but as a part of the wider communities which are the state, the nation, and the world. The comparative study of communities has proved highly successful.

In order for teachers to gain confidence in the values and possibilities of a structured curriculum, it is recommended that they study the implementation of certain well planned programs that can be found in the literature.

---

[10] John D. McAulay, "Some Map Abilities of Second Grade Children," *The Journal of Geography*, Vol. 51 (Jan. 1962), pp. 3–9.

[11] Haig A. Rushdoony, "Achievement in Map-reading: An Experimental Study," *The Elementary School Journal*, Vol. 64 (Nov. 1963), pp. 70–75.

Extending the Program to the Upper Grades

4

Extending the Program to the Upper Grades

It was advocated in the preceding chapter that the community be the central focus or the main theme for study in the primary grades. Within the context of such a theme, young children are able to begin, at least, to understand basic concepts from all social sciences and to be impressed with the reality of interdependence among people. At the same time, it is hoped that the conceptualization method becomes implanted in children and that by the end of the third grade it has started to become their own approach to the social studies.

By the time the children reach the fourth grade and as they go on to the fifth and sixth grades, their ability to read increasingly difficult material, and to read it faster, opens new horizons to them, and their curiosity should be increasingly challenged.

The purpose of this chapter is to provide a central theme for the upper grades of the elementary school and a sequential program which would be justified in view of the changed nature of children in this age group as well as in view of the recent developments in social studies education.

The main theme

Traditionally the social studies content for the upper grades of the elementary school consisted of the state or broad geographical regions of the world for the fourth grade, the United States for the fifth grade, and the rest of the world for the sixth grade. Generally speaking, the program could remain the same, but it should be given a new direction in terms of an overall theme, its sequence, and the conceptualization approach.

The nature of the world and the present role of the United States in this world should dictate the central theme. The world is small and interdependent. What is happening in the most remote areas of the globe affects us considerably. The world is united in terms of communication, transportation, and fear for the future. Major world powers with opposing goals must cooperate with each other in certain respects, because the expansion of conflicts might bring war which could destroy all of them. The world is also divided in a way that unites peoples and nations in favor of or against an ideology, an economic alliance or a defense alliance.

The United States is a world power and as such she has assumed certain responsibilities and has made certain commitments around the world. American men are called upon to serve, fight and even die in far away places. The world needs America and America needs the world. The American people live in a prosperous country, but as a moral people they cannot ignore the problems of the rest of the world. Also, the United States faces certain internal problems which determine the image of this country abroad.

Obviously, one cannot be a good American or a good citizen in today's world without a general understanding of some of the major realities of the world as a whole. Neither the state nor the nation can be taught in isolation.

For these reasons a global concept of the relationships of men should be the main theme for the social studies program in the upper grades of the elementary school. To achieve this global concept, a specific program is suggested in the following pages. This program does not eliminate the elements of the old program. It simply puts them in a more meaningful sequence and provides for a sounder structure.

The first step: Overall view of the world

In order to create the proper setting for the study of any culture or country, it is suggested that the fourth-grade program begin with units attempting to give the child an overall view of the world; to provide him with a framework within which he can place the study of any particular part of the globe. Three major units are suggested for the achievement of this end:

1. The globe from a physical point of view
2. Forces which unite the peoples of the world
3. Forces which divide the peoples of the world

Basically, this program is not a complete departure from the old fourth-grade program which dealt with the regions of the world. The old program, however, approached the study of the world from the climatic and vegetative points of view rather than trying to give a comprehensive picture of the world as it is today. The first unit suggested above, is probably a close repetition of the old program. Units two and three, however, broaden the scope of the program into aspects of human activity beyond those related to climate and terrain.

The physical world. In considering the first unit, the teacher should first take into account the knowledge which the children gained in the primary grades through the generalizations about geography selected for that level. These generalizations are:

1. Life on the earth is influenced by the earth's (global) shape, its size, and its set of motions.
2. Soils are altered by nature and man. Nature combines the action of climate, vegetation, and animals on parent materials to produce regional variations in soils.
3. Man constantly seeks to satisfy his needs for food, clothing and shelter and his other wants; in so doing, he attempts to adapt, shape, utilize, and exploit the earth.

Whatever the children learned in connection with these generalizations can be expanded and directed towards the understanding of the system of relationships upon which the life of any particular living organism is based. Such a system, referred to by geographers as an ecosystem, includes such factors as food supply, weather, and natural enemies.

Another concept for which the children should gain a clear understanding is habitat. The meaning of this concept is closely related to
the meaning which is associated with the term ecosystem. Habitat
refers to a particular ecosystem which in many ways has been changed
by man's planned or casual actions.

There is a limited number of major habitats around the world
and their consideration provides an overall picture of the globe.
Furthermore, an understanding of the relationships between natural
elements, resources, and man gives the background for understanding
the various ways men live and for developing an insight into the
group movements of man and his present and past conflicts.

No specific mention is made of the various habitats because there
appears to be a disagreement as to their number. They range any-
where from three to nine. Some authorities even prefer to avoid the
division of the world in terms of habitats and place more emphasis
on cultures. Cultures and habitats, however, are interrelated. Teachers
should look upon them as such regardless of what source they use to
determine the major divisions of the world.

All that is suggested for study thus far may serve as the basis for
the development of additional generalizations from geography. The
following generalizations are suggested:

1. The evolution of makind from isolated, self-sufficient communities to an interdependent whole, means even more trade,
   migration, diffusion of ideas and practices, and greater importance of relative location or situation.
2. Each culture tends to view its physical habitat differently.
   A society's value system, goals, organization, and level of
   technology determine which elements of the land are prized
   and utilized.
3. Every region is an area homogeneous in terms of specific
   criteria chosen to delimit from other regions. This delimitation
   is always based on an intellectual judgment.[1]

The forces which unite the world. Evidence presented in connection
with the first generalization listed above could serve as the basis to
launch a unit on the forces which unite the world.

Leften Stavrianos and his associates[2] identify the following forces

---

[1] Jan O. M. Broeck, *Geography: Its Scope and Spirit* (Columbus, Ohio: Charles
E. Merrill Books, Inc., 1965), p. 86.
[2] Leften S. Stavrianos *et al, A Global History of Man* (Boston: Allyn and Bacon,
Inc., 1962), pp. 734–740.

which unite the world: transportation facilities, communication facilities, economic interdependence, and common ways of life.

It is in connection with this unit that the children will become aware of economic alliances, such as the European Common Market, and the reasons for which such alliances were formed. The various military or defense alliances can be justified at this point in terms of their goal to defend and protect the various ways of life. The concept of interdependence ought to be the main focus in the study of this unit.

The study of the uniting forces should be concluded with the consideration of the United Nations. It is suggested that the teachers avoid overburdening the students with memorizing the mammoth structure of this organization. Instead they should capitalize on the role of the United Nations in resolving specific international conflicts and in assisting underdeveloped nations to improve educationally, socially, and economically. The study of the United Nations could serve as an effective means to bring to the children's awareness some of the most significant world problems such as the population explosion, food shortages in most parts of the globe, and disease epidemics.

Generalizations introduced earlier should always be strengthened with the study of any unit. The study of the forces which unite the world could contribute to the development of a broader and deeper meaning for many of the generalizations listed in connection with other units. Listed below are examples of new generalizations which could be introduced at this point:

1. The world is shrinking in distance and time—information can be transmitted around the globe at once and transportation between nations and continents is much faster than ever before.
2. Food, clothing, and shelter are needs of all human beings.
3. A knowledge of cultures of other nations contributes to better communication and international understanding.
4. The recognition of human rights and human dignity is basic to personal relationships and to government.[3]

The forces which divide the world. An anlysis of the voting patterns of the United Nations could very well lead into this unit about the forces which divide the world.

---

[3] Harold M. Long and Robert N. King, *Improving the Teaching of World Affairs —The Glens Falls Story*, Bulletin No. 35 (Washington, D.C.: The National Council for the Social Studies, 1964), pp. 30–31.

Some of the same forces which unite the peoples of the world in large associations are also the forces which keep these associations apart from each other. For instance, there is more diffusion between the different ways of life today and this brings the world closer together, but the existence of different ways of life is in itself a dividing force. The students should be introduced into the relatively few major ways of life around the world.

Economic interdependence brought the nations together, but also divided them in terms of economic blocs competing with each other. The need for peace brought people to international cooperation, but a need for national security forced them into defense blocs such as the North Atlantic Treaty Organization, the Warsaw Pact and many others.

Race, religion and language differences and certain historical developments have been causes for dividing the world, but the most important dividing cause is the present ideological struggle which created three major camps: the free world, the communist world, and the neutral nations which do not desire to attach themselves to either side.

In spite of the fact that this unit deals with the forces which divide the world, the teaching of it should be focused on generalizations which give an overall picture of an interdependent world. Some generalizations to be introduced and developed here could be:

1. People of all races, religions, and cultures have contributed to the cultural heritage. Modern society owes a debt to cultural innovators of other places and times.
2. All human beings are of one biological species within which occur negligible variations.[4]

The second step: The United States of America

Giving an overall view of the world early in the upper grades satisfies the children's interests and provides them with a general background which will enable them to study meaningfully, smaller parts of the globe or specific cultures. Any cultural region could be

---

[4] California State Department of Education, "Report of the State Central Committee on Social Studies," in: Byron G. Massialas and Andreas M. Kazamias, *Crucial Issues in the Teaching of Social Studies* (Englewood Cliffs, N. J.: Prentice-Hall, Inc., 1964), pp. 62–63.

introduced at this point. In many respects, however, the study of the United States appears as the most logical step to be taken.

To begin with, the children are interested in their own country and they want to know more about it. Listening and reading about their own country is an everyday thing and it generates many questions to which the children wish answers.

In the traditional program the study of the United States was placed in the fifth grade. In the suggested sequence it falls at approximately the same level. This is good in view of the fact that most of the materials on the United States which were written for elementary school children are geared towards the fifth-grade level.

In studying the people of the United States, one studies the people of many nations who came to this country to live in peace and try to achieve some degree of prosperity. The people of this country could serve as excellent avenues to the study of other cultures. All societies or cultures have approximately the same needs. The difference between various societies or cultures lies in the ways these needs are satisfied. Knowledge of the way in which the societal needs are satisfied in the United States gives a basis for comparison in the study of other societies and cultures. This provides for a logical sequence since, in the same manner, knowledge of the way in which local community needs are satisfied gave a basis for the study of the same needs on a national scale.

Some important considerations. Suggesting to the teachers that the next step should be to teach about the United States is not enough. Important considerations should be brought to their attention to enable them to avoid some of the mistakes of the past and make teaching about the United States more realistic.

Teachers and curriculum workers, when faced with the task of developing a syllabus on the United States, wonder if their approach should be primarily geographical, historical or focused on current problems and issues. Most likely neither one of these approaches is the best, because selection of one of them will mean underemphasis of the other two.

The approach to be used should be dictated by the purpose of the subject and by the nature of those for whom the subject is intended. A very small percentage of the millions of children in the elementary schools will become experts in some aspect of American History or

Geography or the American way of life. What the masses of children need is not a throughly detailed study of their country but a comprehensive and general picture of it. They need a common sense understanding of the relationships between the land and the people, of the various ways of life which the American people have and how these ways of life have developed. In an approach such as this, knowledge from all social science disciplines is equally important.

The interdisciplinary approach, therefore, as some sources refer to it, is probably the best approach for the study not only of the United States, but of any unit on the globe.

Some teachers approach the study of the United States from a chronological point of view. They start with the colonial days, or even before that, and move through the Revolution to the Civil War and post Civil War era, and then to the twentieth century. By the end of the year, they enter into the Second World War, but there is not enough time to relate all this knowledge to the present.

It is strongly recommended that at this level, the understanding of the contemporary American scene should be the primary objective. The past should be studied only as a means to understand the present. Such an approach will inevitably provide numerous opportunities to bring the past into focus. For example, the student who is considering the differences between the North and the South will get a better insight by referring to the Civil War. The student who is disturbed by the present relationships between the United States and Latin America can find some explanations by studying the past. The past by itself is gone, and interesting mostly to the historian, but its importance is vital for all when it is used to interpret the present.

Textbooks in general and American History textbooks in particular have been criticized for many reasons. The gravest criticism probably has been that of bias and misrepresentation which were present not only in early textbooks, but in those that are presently in use as well. As late as the 1930's the textbooks were advocating the superiority of the Anglo-Saxons and the inferiority of the Southern and Southeastern Europeans.[5] Even to the very present the Negro is much

---

[5] Edward N. Saveth, "Good Stocks and Lesser Breeds," in: Arthur Foff and Jean D. Gramb, *Readings in Education* (New York: Harper and Brothers, 1956), pp. 281–287.

neglected. Studies of American History textbooks indicate that "many textbooks either distort or omit important information on the history and achievements of the Negroes."[6]

The American society is composed of many groups which must tolerate each other and continue to live together. Bias and misrepresentation lead to prejudice and unfounded conclusions which make democracy unworkable and good life an impossibility.

One thing which should always be in the mind of each teacher while planning a program on the United States, is the fact that, like any other nation, it is a part of a very interdependent world. We should teach the youngsters not only how we influence other nations and cultures, but how other nations and cultures influence our way of life. We depend upon them in the same way they depend upon us. People in other parts of the world want evidence that we respect them and appreciate their contributions whatever they are. The youngsters should be made to feel proud of the scientific and technological advances which the American people have made, but they should also be made aware of the contributions of the Germans, Russians, Japanese and others. After all, the roots of American culture are Greek and Roman civilizations, Judeo-Christian religion, the English law and language, and the good qualities of the people who came here from many other nations.

Another very important consideration should be to provide an integration between what has been learned in the previous grades and what is being taught about the United States. The conceptualization approach advocated all through this book makes this integration possible. Most of the generalizations which served as the basis for the study of the community and for providing an overall understanding of the world could serve as the integrating agents. The study of the United States can be based on most of the same generalizations.

To illustrate this point the following example is used: In the preceding chapter it was shown how a particular generalization could be developed in the primary grades. The generalization used as an example was, "National migration develops cultural diversity within a group and cultural diffusion among groups." In the study of the

---

[6] Board of Education of the City of New York, *The Negro in American History* (New York: The Board of Education of the City of New York, 1964), p. v.

United States the meaning of this generalization could be extended through the study of the immigration movement to the United States, the policies associated with it and the effects which immigration has had and continues to have upon American society.

No attempt is being made here to identify those generalizations from the primary grades which lend themselves more to providing the necessary integration. Since all primary grade generalizations contribute in some degree to this end, each teacher should make his or her own selection.

Additional generalizations and important topics. Teaching about the United States should not be limited by the generalizations provided through the primary grades curriculum. Additional generalizations should be identified to assist in the achievement of very important objectives such as the development of a commitment to democracy. Among the additional generalizations the following could be included:

1. In the United States democracy is dependent on the process of free inquiry.
2. The basic substance of a society is rooted in its values; assessing the nature of those values is the most persistent and important problem faced by human beings.
3. Democracy is based on such beliefs as the integrity of man, the dignity of the individual, equality of opportunity, man's rationality, man's morality, man's ability to govern himself and to solve his problems cooperatively.[7]

There is no question that generalizations such as the ones listed above are pregnant with rich topics and provide for an interdisciplinary approach. Each teacher should allow her knowledge about the United States, her degree of commitment to the American ideals and her role in today's societal problems to make the decision as to what topics should be stressed more. However, the contemporary American scene demands that certain topics be dealt with by necessity. These topics are:

1. The history of the Negro in America, and the effects of slavery, reconstruction and segregation upon current racial problems.

---

[7] California State Department of Education, "Report of the State Central Committee on Social Studies," in: Byron G. Massialas and Andreas M. Kazamias, *Crucial Issues in the Teaching of Social Studies* (Englewood Cliffs, N.J.: Prentice-Hall, Inc., 1964), p. 62.

2. The history of other minority groups and their assimilation into American Society. These groups would include Italians, Poles, Orientals, Jews, Mexicans, Puerto Ricans.
3. The rise of the city, and resulting urban and surburban problems.
4. The role of labor, management and government in determining labor-managment-consumer relations.
5. Changing interpretations of Civil Rights, and the growing responsibility of the federal government in their enforcement.

In selecting specific topics to foster the same generalizations all through the program, Paul Hanna's basic social functions which were presented in the second chapter should not be overlooked. Like the generalizations, the basic social functions will contribute to the continuity of the program. The nature of the basic social functions is the same at the local community level and at the national level. The difference lies in their operation and the problems associated with it.

While the generalizations and the topics suggested will be a focus to give direction, the main objective at this level should be a general understanding by the children of the country and the society in which they live.

The third step: An Asian or African culture

By this time the children have dealt with the community and it is hoped that they have gained an understanding of their national way of life and how it came to be what it is. They learned of the basic social functions by referring to their own community and nation, and they became aware of their role in the better operation of these functions. Also, they have been exposed to the world-wide setting of which their community and their nation is an integral part.

The time left before the children go to the junior high school is rather short and must be used as wisely as possible. In the past, the sixth-grade program consisted mostly of studies related to the European continent or the Latin American countries. The children had no opportunity to be exposed to an Asian or African culture. It is suggested here that in order for the program to meet the criterion of comprehensiveness within the existing time limits, the sixth-grade social studies program should concentrate on either Africa, Asia or both.

This suggestion does not imply that Europe and Latin America are not important. They are very important, but proper treatment of the United States would by necessity touch upon Europe and Latin America. The majority of the people in the United States are of European origin and no good teacher would avoid referring to Europe and European life while studying the American people. The United States and its history are interrelated with the Latin American countries and their history to the extent that proper understanding of the United States cannot be conceived apart from the rest of the continent.

It is true that Europe and Latin America are indirectly and not adequately treated. Nevertheless, the children do study western culture through the study of the United States. It appears logical that they should end their elementary school education by being exposed to one or two completely different cultures such as an Asian and African culture.

The teacher should be the one to decide if she will teach one or two cultures. In either case she should avoid the old-fashioned country-by-country coverage. Generalizations should be taught and not countries, though a country may be used as the vehicle. The children have already been exposed to the forces which divide the world, but it would be advisable to start the teaching of a culture by identifying those general elements which make this particular culture unique.

The basic social functions should be used to provide a comprehensive coverage of a culture. What are the organizational problems in Africa, for instance, and how do governments emerge and operate? What is the status of production and distribution of goods and services? How do Africans provide for education and how important is education? By making the basic social functions the basis for the study of a culture, some of the same generalizations used for the study of the community and the United States could apply here as well.

While pointing out the differences between cultures is informative, the need to educate the students about the interaction and diffusion among cultures is imperative. The attitude of acceptance and tolerance of different ways of life should be developed at all times.

It should be emphasized that the primary concern of the elementary teacher should be to provide a common sense understanding of the present world. The traditional approach of spending most of the children's time and effort in memorizing various dynasties of the past should be avoided. The past should be utilized only to the extent it is needed to make the present more meaningful and the concept of the global relationships of men more comprehensible.

The development of skills in the upper grades

Whatever was said about the development of skills in connection with the primary grades applies to the upper grades as well. The upper grades are the ground for practice to make the skills a matter of habit in the everyday affairs of children.

Through this chapter the importance of developing generalizations has been stressed. It should be added here that the skills and the total process involved in the development of the generalizations are of equal importance. The children should gain an understanding of the world today, but the world changes and it will change in many ways in the lifetime of the children. Old generalizations will have to be modified or give way entirely to new generalizations. The children should capitalize on the skills of critical thinking and evaluation so that they can understand, accept, and adapt themselves to these changes. There are those who claim that the process of evaluating generalizations is of more importance as an educational objective than learning the generalizations themselves.

Children were exposed to map making and reading in the primary grades. In the upper grades the children should be made aware of the vast variety of maps and learn how to use them. Teachers are urged to become thoroughly familiar themselves with all these maps. Their quality and their apparent usefulness generates a moving enthusiasm of which no teacher or classroom should be deprived.

Time and zone concepts were regarded beyond the grasp of elementary children. Recent research shows that children can understand these concepts if they are properly taught. Teachers should familiarize themselves with the related literature and attempt to find ways for the better teaching of these difficult concepts. The utilization of maps and globes becomes very important in this regard.

In the primary grades, charts, graphs, cartoons and other graphic and symbolic materials are used mostly for the purpose of understanding their nature. In the upper grades their use becomes what it should be, the tools through which the youngsters organize and interpret cognitive content for better understanding.

SUMMARY

The main theme in the primary grades is community studies. In a small and interdependent world such as ours, the main theme for the upper grades should be a global understanding. In order to achieve this end within the existing time limits and without completely changing the old program, a specific sequential program is suggested.

The first unit is designed to give an overall understanding of the world in terms of the physical characteristics of the earth and the way they affect men, the forces which unite the peoples of the world and the forces which divide them. This type of world picture will provide the student with a framework within which he can study any culture.

The American culture should be studied first because it is obviously of vital importance to the child and because he is interested in learning about his country. It is easier for the child and the teacher to start with the culture in which they live and then use it as the basis for the study of other cultures.

Asia, Africa or both are recommended to be studied next in some detail instead of Europe or Latin America. This is necessary to provide for a comprehensive knowledge of the world. The cultures of Europe and Latin America are western, like our own, and do not present the sharp contrast to American life that Asian and African cultures do.

The basic social functions should be the basis for the study of each culture. Structure and continuity all through the elementary grades should be provided through the further development of the same generalizations. New generalizations will also have to be introduced as the program advances.

As in the primary grades, the development of commitments on the part of the children should not be avoided. Appropriate skills should be further developed through their use in the understanding and application of cognitive content.

Planning for Instruction: The Unit and the Lesson Plans

5

Planning for Instruction:
The Unit and the
Lesson Plans

The unit and the lesson plans as presented in this chapter reflect the method of conceptualization, and, taking into consideration the individual differences of children, provide for a way of teaching which makes use of a variety of resources and activities.

A. The unit plan

IN NEED OF A NEW APPROACH

When someone deals in theory it is impossible to advocate any other method of teaching social studies to young children than the method inherent in the unit plan. Quite often, however, teachers who return to colleges and universities to take refresher courses laugh at the education professors who so strongly anathematize the use of one textbook and put themselves 100 percent in favor of the unit plan. The teachers know that in practice the majority of them continue to teach from one textbook and that in all probability they will continue to do so in the future.

Certainly this is a disturbing phenomenon, but in most cases the situation is such not because the teachers are unconvinced of the superiority of the unit plan, but mainly because it is difficult for them to abandon the textbook entirely and at once. Unfortunately, this is what they have been asked to do since the unit plan emerged. They were asked to take a big jump to reach an end quite remote from their original base. Such a daring and impractical suggestion was rejected and continues to be rejected. In view of this rejection there is need for a new approach to help the teachers to move away from the textbook and towards the unit plan in a manner which is gradual and more realistic. This new approach constitutes the basic characteristic of this chapter.

It is assumed that in-service teachers are familiar with the theoretical arguments for abandoning the textbook in favor of unit teaching. Therefore, the presentation of these arguments is brief and simply serves as an introduction followed by a rather extensive description of the structure of the unit plan. This description is deemed necessary in view of the existing variety of forms of the unit plan. The teachers should know the end toward which they are aiming. The chapter closes with a brief consideration of the lesson plan and its relationship to the unit plan.

Why Abandon the Textbook?

Teachers and educators in general often become unnecessarily fanatic over issues which have not yet been resolved. For example, research cannot support the phonics method of teaching reading as superior to the "look and say" method. Both methods are just as effective under the proper circumstances. Yet, some teachers and even reading supervisors are completely against one of these methods and in favor of the other. When it comes to the issue of whether to abandon the textbook in favor of the unit plan, however, and especially in the teaching of social studies, there seems to be no doubt as to what is the right thing to do. The textbook, as it is used, is simply inadequate and the reasons for this are many.

It was pointed out elsewhere in this book that social studies deals with human relationships and that human relationships today mean, for the most part, conflicts. Undoubtedly, the best way to deal with human conflicts is to present all sides and help the youngsters to think about them with an open mind. The use of one textbook cannot achieve this. The author of a textbook, intentionally or not, will tend to bias the thinking of the youngsters regardless of how much he might have tried to be objective. In many cases publishers of textbooks are forced by local or sectional conditions and pressures to be less objective than they would normally desire to be or to avoid dealing adequately with certain areas of study. It was reported recently, for example, that the Negro is alarmingly omitted from American History textbooks used widely across the nation. While the publishers were probably forced to make this omission, the teachers can, if they wish, make up for it.

Furthermore, the use of one textbook contradicts the most peculiar characteristic of the American education system. This characteristic is the diversity and wide range of abilities present in each grade level. From the teacher's point of view this is a gigantic problem. In many parts of the world where education is by necessity or by design the privilege of the few, this problem is solved by creating homogeneous groups through the elimination of many children from the educative process. In the United States this cannot and should not take place, because it is the birthright of everyone to have the opportunity to have an education and to advance that education to the maximum. It is not right under these circumstances to force every child in a particular grade to follow one textbook written for the average child in that grade. Those who do, lose the youngsters with below average ability and bore those who have above average ability.

Besides the individual differences in children there are also the sectional and environmental differences which make the use of one textbook inadequate. Children living in the city, for instance, should emphasize in their studies the farm more than the children living on farms, and vice versa. Children in New York need to study more about oil than children in Texas. Unless the teachers depart from the use of one textbook these adjustments cannot be made.

Another objection to the use of a single textbook in the teaching of social studies is the fact that they rapidly become outdated. Occasionally, texts are outdated in certain respects as soon as they are published. It is impossible for them to keep up with the rapid and often significant changes in today's world.

Unit Plan the Best Alternative

In order to make up for the inadequacies of the textbook and bring the teachers' practices in line with the modern concept of teaching, the unit plan appears to be the best alternative. According to John Dewey[1] teaching means making children think. Thinking is sensing a problem, collecting and evaluating pertinent information, hypothesizing, testing the hypothesis, and reaching conclusions. It is upon this process of thinking or problem solving, as some refer to it, that the unit plan is structured. It is a way of teaching consistent with the best modern theories of learning. The conceptualization approach in teaching which lately has fascinated educators across the nation and stimulated a considerable amount of research and experimentation is a strong guiding factor in unit teaching as presented in this chapter. Furthermore, and as it will be illustrated later, unit planning and teaching constitute a strong link between the school and the community because the community is involved in the actual teaching process.

In order for unit teaching to produce satisfactory results it should be done properly. Unfortunately, however, in many classrooms a number of time-wasting schemes are justified under the pretext of unit teaching. Some teachers make the mistake of considering an isolated field trip with loose objectives or an isolated project as being the same as a unit. Others spend too much time on units which they like the most at the expense of a comprehensive and balanced program. Poor unit teaching is probably worse than non-unit teaching. It is for this reason that a rather detailed description of the structure of the unit plan is considered necessary.

The Structure of the Unit Plan

Various textbooks and journal articles present the form of the unit plan by listing the structural elements of this plan. A variation in these lists is evident and, to the person not familiar with the unit plan, this is confusing. Actually there are no substantial differences

---

[1] John Dewey, *Democracy and Education* (New York: The Macmillan Company, 1916), p. 192.

from one form to the other. If one attempts to carefully analyze seemingly different forms of unit plans, he will discover, possibly with no exception, that three basic elements are always present. These elements are the objectives to be achieved, the content and its presentation, or the means and the ways through which these objectives can be achieved, and the techniques of evaluation or the ways the teacher finds out if the children are reaching or have reached the objectives. Everything else in the structure of a unit constitutes some part in these three basic structural elements or serves some kind of an auxiliary function.

Due to the practical nature of this book, an attempt has been made to present the structure of the unit plan in a practical sequence, that is, the sequence which the teacher should follow in preparing a unit for her class.

The title. The first thing which a teacher has to do before starting a new school year is to decide upon the titles of the units which she is going to teach. This is not easy because there is much to be taught in a limited period of time. All American History, for example, might have to be taught in one grade. Time would not permit the study of too many details and the teachers have to be selective. The events which had the greatest impact upon the development of the American nation and the most basic issues, concepts and generalizations should be selected. Failure to do this will lead to overstressing one aspect of American History while neglecting, or just touching upon, other aspects equally or even more important.

As soon as the titles are determined the teacher should prepare a folder for each title and alert herself to materials which can be placed in these folders. Anything related to the topics is good at this stage. They should include lists of books, book reviews, magazine and newspaper articles, pictures, maps, graphs, lists of films and filmstrips, pamphlets and other items. These folders when properly applied can be used year after year.

When the time comes for the teacher to teach a specific unit the appropriate folder will serve as the base from which to start. First she will review the materials to familiarize herself with the topic. Definitely she should go beyond these materials to make herself as comfortable as possible with the content. Otherwise, limited knowledge will control the teacher and tend to limit her enthusiasm in presenting the unit.

It should be emphasized in connection with the title that the same units should not be taught year after year. Certain conditions might demand some changes within a general framework. For years a teacher was probably teaching a unit on Thailand when dealing with southeast Asia. Viet Nam would probably be a better choice under the present conditions.

The objectives. The next task in planning a unit is determining the objectives. Objectives mean the specific changes to be achieved in the three domains of the individual as defined in the first chapter. These domains are the cognitive, the affective and the psychomotor. In determining the objectives, questions such as the following should be asked: What concepts should be developed? What generalizations or conclusions should the youngsters reach? What outlook towards their objects of study should they develop? Are there any attitudes or dispositions that should be changed or developed in children through the study of a particular unit? Do they need to develop any specific skills in order to be able to successfully proceed in the study of this and other topics? When the answers to these questions become the objectives, everything the children study is oriented towards helping them in their everyday life or is considered fundamental in enabling them to better cope with future studies. The acquisition of isolated facts alone cannot accomplish this, because facts are meaningless unless they are seen as parts of broader understandings. The facts about China developing a hydrogen bomb or her not belonging to the United Nations, for example, are by themselves not important. They assume, though, great importance when they are integrated with other knowledge of China to determine what impact she is going to have upon the future of the world.

In planning a unit on China, then, the objective is not only the acquisition of the aforementioned facts, but the reaching of conclusions or the developing of an understanding of the impact which China might have upon the future of the world. Such an understanding is an important objective not only in that each child will be a part of the future world, but also, from the point of view that it will help children gain further understanding of the behavior of other nations.

When instruction increases the power of the learners in these terms it obviously changes their behavior.

A unit must have structure and to provide it the objectives should be derived from a limited number of basic generalizations as developed by social scientists. When these generalizations are interpreted into subgeneralizations, affective objectives (values and attitudes), and skills (social and intellectual), they provide the objectives of the unit. It is assumed that by achieving these objectives the children will have developed the generalizations to some extent.

Deriving the objectives from generalizations naturally reflects an emphasis on the importance of the disciplines. It also points to another new direction which eliminates a misunderstanding. Years ago, if someone went to a classroom in September and asked a teacher what her objectives were for the year, she might have answered that she would not know the answer to that question until June. The era is gone in which the children's immediate needs and interests alone determined the objectives of instruction. The teacher, not the children, is most qualified to determine the objectives. She knows the interests of children as well as their present and future needs. At the same time, she has an adequate knowledge of the structure and the basic elements of the disciplines from which the elementary school social studies are drawn. At the elementary school level, the role of the school should be geared more towards the future than the present. In the majority of cases, home can take care of the present.

If, in the past, the needs and interests of children were given so much weight in determining the objectives, it was due to the prominence which certain psychological principles received in the teaching-learning process. Psychologists insisted that learning is facilitated and becomes more permanent if the children feel a need for, and are interested in, what they learn. This is true, but in order for the schools to apply important psychological principles such as the ones mentioned, they do not have to throw structured learnings out. Good teaching can generate need as well as interest in any learning. It is suggested, therefore, that the teacher should prepare the objectives as suggested and through her clever techniques make the children discover and adopt these objectives.

An additional point related to the objectives should be made clear. Objectives are often divided into general and specific. The specific objectives were defined in the preceding paragraphs. In the past, the general objectives in a social studies unit plan were in most cases the objectives of the social studies in general. Consequently, they were the same from one unit to the other. Their function was to keep the randomly selected specific objectives and the study of each unit within the general scope of the social studies. They formed the general framework within which the elementary school teacher functioned as a social studies teacher.

With the emphasis of social studies now directed more toward the disciplines and their structure, the nature of general objectives has changed. Instead of the usual broad and often vague statements which were formulated by teachers' committees, they represent those generalizations from the social sciences which serve as the sources from which specific objectives are derived. The generalizations which were considered appropriate for the implementation of the program suggested in this book are to be found in the third and fourth chapters. Those which appear to be closely related to the various topics should be selected for each unit. The number of generalizations could vary from unit to unit but there should not be too many of them. Also, it should not be expected that all generalizations listed in a unit should be developed completely. It takes time, and some of them might have to be repeated in other units.

Problems and activities. The objectives set the direction the development of a unit must take. The means are now needed to assist in following this direction. It is at this stage that the value of the content is very obvious. Many sources suggest that the content should be outlined here in considerable detail. This suggestion, however, would be useful if the teacher were to lecture to the class. But good teaching in the elementary school is not lecturing; it is, instead, providing the children with problems both interesting and basic to the topic under consideration and then directing them in finding by themselves the solutions or answers to these problems.

What is needed, therefore, in the place of an outline is the content converted into a number of basic problems. These problems should be basic questions to which the answers should lead to the formulation of important relationships. The relationships should represent the objectives.

To return to an earlier illustration, in order to enable the children to understand that China will have a great impact upon the world in the near future, several basic problems or questions to which the students might address themselves are: "Through what means do the leaders of Communist China claim that they should help achieve the goal of communizing the world?" "What was the reaction of the world to the explosion of the first atom bomb by the Chinese?" It is emphasized again that adequate knowledge of the subject matter in connection with any unit will be the only means to secure a list of more fundamental problems. Recent books written by subject matter specialists should be consulted in order that modern trends in various fields not be neglected. Value questions should also be raised.

In a plan developed from a practical point of view, detailed activities to go with each problem are necessary and constitute a very important and integral part of the unit. The activities spell out the class-period by class-period and day-by-day course of action the children will follow under the direction of the teacher in dealing intelligently with the designated problems. While the overall unit plan represents the broader method of teaching, the activities represent the techniques of teaching.

In order for the teacher to function satisfactorily at this point she should be very familiar with and take into consideration two additional factors besides the subject matter problems. These factors are the nature of the children as individuals and as a group, and the various teaching resources which are related and can be applied. The teacher should know the general ability and the experiential background of the children, but most of all she should thoroughly diagnose the children's knowledge of the particular topic to be studied. It helps to avoid unnecessary repetition for some youngsters, and it helps identify members of the class who can be used as motivating agents.

Resources related to the social studies include the community, the trade books and other reading materials, the various audio-visual aids, current events, maps and globes and various dramatic and rhythmic exercises. All these can be utilized to make the study of social studies or the search for answers to basic problems a very vivid and realistic experience. These resources provide various avenues leading towards the same objectives; each child can follow the avenue of his convenience. Activities can be found for the slow child which are less abstract than those designated for the gifted child. The significant thing is that all activities lead to some degree of realization of the same goals. In other words, the utilization of the various teaching resources provides for the individual differences. At the same time it allows for more than one viewpoint in controversial matters.

The most convenient way to record the problems and activities of a unit is to divide sheets of paper into two columns and record the problems in one column and the activities in the other as follows:

PROBLEMS	ACTIVITIES
A.	1. ....
	2. ....
B. Through what means do the leaders of Communist China claim that they will help achieve the goal of communizing the rest of the world?	1. Direct the students to analyze speeches by Chinese leaders.
	2. Have them read of the dispute between China and Russia and then have a discussion.
	3. Direct them to the appropriate sources to find out the reasons for which China was not admitted to the United Nations.
C. What was the reaction of the world to the development of the hydrogen bomb by China?	1. Have children bring to the class as many reactions as they can find in back newspapers and magazines.
	2. Display the clippings and point out the general agreement as to the increase of the prestige and influence of China.
	3. Illustrate the influence of China upon other nations using Cambodia and Indonesia as examples.
D.	1. ....

This form is probably the most convenient one because it is easy to follow from one day to the next. A substitute teacher will have no difficulty following it because the activities spell out in detail what should be done in connection with each problem. The activities will not have to be reworked as happens when they are stated in very general terms.

In the example of the arrangement of problems and activities just cited children used reading, discussion, reviewing current events and displaying as activities. There are many more types of activities that can be used while taking advantage of the various resources that were mentioned earlier. They range from the most concrete, for the slow child, to the most abstract, for the gifted child. Wilhelmina Hill gives the following rather extensive list of activities:

1. Reading for information . . .
2. Viewing informational films and filmstrips.
3. Listening to recordings and people.
4. Carrying out experiments.
5. Taking notes on needed information.
6. Studying maps and globes.
7. Taking field trips to gather information.
8. Making collections.
9. Writing letters for information.
10. Interviewing appropriate people.
11. Studying pictures for information.
12. Reading the landscape for geographic information.
13. Discussing unit problems and progress.
14. Sharing information in small and large groups.
15. Keeping a record of information each child is gathering.
16. Organizing information on charts and graphs.[2]

There are many more that a clever teacher can think of and design.

Another merit of unit teaching should be pointed out at this point. It provides for an unknown number of indirect learnings. It is perfectly clear that while a youngster is searching the various resources for an answer he is being indirectly exposed to a considerable amount of information. Some of it might arouse his curiosity and challenge him to further reading. Some of it might clear previous misconceptions. At the same time this design of teaching allows for the development of social studies skills in a functional manner. There is no better way to develop skills. Many teachers use the wrong approach in developing skills. For example, it is possible to find teachers who set

---

[2] Wilhelmina Hill, *Social Studies in the Elementary School Program*, Bulletin No. 5 (Washington, D.C.: U.S. Office of Education, 1960), p. 50.

aside time for the teaching of the problem solving method, but who do not use it as their method of instruction. Teaching children this way is like giving instruction to a group of undernourished people on proper diet without giving them the necessary food. Children cannot be told to be cooperative. Cooperativeness and all other skills and attitudes necessary for a democratic way of life develop in situations which children see as real life situations. A good unit plan is nothing more than a well designed sequence of such situations.

Initiation and culminating activities. The initiating and the culminating of the unit plan constitute the first and the last activities in the execution of the unit. These two activities are considered separately because of the special function which they perform and because they do not directly relate to any one of the specific subject matter problems.

Even though the teacher decides in advance what the objectives, the problems, and to a great extent the activities of a unit will be, she must have a planning session with the children in which to motivate them to study the unit and direct them to the adoption of her plans. After this session the children should be left with the feeling that they want to study about the particular unit topic and that the course of action for the study of the unit was decided collectively and not by the teacher alone.

In order that this planning be successful it is desirable to do something which will put the children in the proper mood; in other words, to initiate the unit. This can be done by appealing to their affective domain and arousing their interest in the topic, or by connecting the study of the new topic with previous learnings. Any clever idea will do the job. To present a list of possible initiation activities will probably only limit the imagination of the individual teacher. One or two examples, however, should be cited. A unit on Africa, for example, can be initiated by showing a film on African life. Then drums, probably made by another class, may be distributed to the children to imitate the playing and dancing seen in the film. Such an activity serves to develop in children an identification with the Africans and discussion about that continent will then be more enthusiastic. The study of the Golden Age of the Greeks, to use another example, can naturally lead to the study of what constitutes a strong and good government, because without the strong and wise leadership of Pericles there might not have been a Golden Age.

Initiation is the opening activity of the unit. There is also a need for a culminating activity or activities. For several days the children were involved in various tasks in reflectively coping with the designated problems. The goals for all the children were the same, but the paths each one of them took to get to these goals were different. The culminating activity or activities give an opportunity to the whole class to reflect collectively and relate everything they studied. Life in Africa, for instance, may be portrayed by a series of dioramas. A study on comparative government may be culminated with the making and displaying of charts depicting the structure of each type of government. Everyone should participate when the unit is culminated. It is rewarding and meaningful for each child to see his work as a part of the total accomplishment of his class. Many times culminating activities may result in an exhibit or a performance to be viewed by the rest of the school and even the parents. It should be stressed, however, that the purpose of culminating activities is not to produce a show or to help teachers gain praise from supervisors and parents. The learnings to be achieved should always be the central focus.

Evaluation. The most important thing to remember in connection with the evaluation of student progress in a unit is that it does not take place only after the teaching of the unit is completed. Evaluation is a part of teaching and it is directed not only towards the children, but towards the teacher as well. Everything the teacher does with her class should have an objective. If she feels that the objective is not reached, she should think the situation over and try to revise her teaching techniques.

Another important rule to remember is that pencil and paper tests are not the only means of evaluation. These tests are of knowledge only, and this is not the total concern of social studies. It includes attitudes, beliefs and skills as well which cannot be measured with ordinary pencil and paper tests. A variety, therefore, of evaluation techniques is necessary. These techniques are described in a later chapter and include observation, group discusion, interviews, checklists, scrapbooks, samples of work and several others.

The techniques of evaluation are not necessarily the same from one unit plan to the next. The nature of the objectives, the content and the activities often indicates the most successful evaluation techniques to be used. The teacher ought to develop an alertness in perceiving these indications and register the appropriate techniques under each unit plan.

Resources. This last section in the structure of the unit plan is like an appendix in which the resources used in the activities are recorded in full detail. They are usually classified as books (for the teacher and for the childen), magazines, pamphlets, newspapers and other printed materials, films and filmstrips, places to visit, persons to be invited to speak to the class and other special resources which might be used.

Working Unit Plan versus Resource Unit Plan

There is little difference between a working unit plan and a resource unit plan. A working unit plan is developed with a specific group of children in mind, while the resource unit plan is developed for any class in a particular grade level or even for any grade within a specific range. This, of course, demands that the resource unit plan provide the teacher with opportunities for choices. For each problem there should be many activities so that the teacher will choose the ones appropriate to her class. There should be more than one initiating activity or culminating activity. All possible techniques of evaluation should be presented in a resource unit. Also, the teacher should suggest all the resources which are available and related to the topic since there is no way of knowing which ones various teachers might need.

Most of the commercial units are resource units. Before they are used, they should be adapted to the intellectual level of a particular class, the needs and interests of the children, and the local environmental differences. A teacher with low ability students, for example, will select mostly concrete activities. A teacher in a farm community will spend less time on the study of the farm or will stress different things than a teacher in the city.

Textbook versus Unit Plan: A Working Compromise

Many good ideas in education were implemented in haste and without a careful plan. Consequently, these ideas did not bring about the anticipated results. For approximately forty years, theorists in

education have glorified the merits of unit teaching; what the teachers were convinced of about unit teaching was not its merits, but its seeming waste of time, loosening of discipline, and lack of subject matter (pages in a textbook). Obviously, a plan is needed to move the teachers away from the textbook gradually so that they can see the merits of the unit plan without loosing at once the security which the textbook gives them.

Such a plan could be comprised of the following steps:

1. In the beginning the teachers could use the textbook to determine the number and the titles of the units to be taught.
2. By considering the local circumstances and the children in the class, the teacher might decide to eliminate a few topics from the ones included in the textbook and add others which she considers more appropriate. This process of elimination and addition of topics will constitute a small but significant step away from the textbook.
3. Also, the textbook could be used to determine the concepts and generalizations to be developed and the specific content problems which will lead to their development. Their validity should be tested.
4. In connection with each content problem the teacher can use various teaching resources along with the textbook. In the beginning it might be only a film or an interesting current article or an exciting book or a set of pictures or a firsthand report, but it will be more than the textbook.
5. As time goes on, more resources will be brought into the teaching process.
6. Eventually other resources will become just as important as the textbook not only in the form of activities, but in the determination of the topics to be taught, the concepts and generalizations to be developed and the specific content problems necessary to develop them. The time will come when the textbook will be another source or it will not be needed at all.

An Example of a Unit Plan

This unit is planned to be used with an upper grade in the elementary school. The children are of average or above average ability. The number of problems is limited in order to save space, but the coverage of the topic is comprehensive. It is supposed to be a working unit, but it was difficult to make it exactly that without a particular class in mind.

The title: CONSERVATION OF NATURAL RESOURCES

OBJECTIVES:

General:

The specific objectives of this unit are based on the following generalizations. The teacher is reminded that these generalizations are not expected to be fully developed by this unit alone.

1. Man constantly seeks to satisfy his needs for food, clothing and shelter and his other wants; in so doing, he attempts to adapt, shape, utilize, and exploit the earth.
2. Each culture tends to view its physical habitat differently. A society's value system, goals, organization, and level of technology determine which elements of the land are prized and utilized.
3. Soils are altered by nature and man. Nature combines the action of climate, vegetation, and animals on parent materials to produce regional variations in soils.

Specific:

1. To enable children to recognize that our lives and the greatness of our nation depend upon the resources we get from nature.
2. To assist the children to understand the interrelatedness of natural resources and to identify the ways in which this interrelatedness can be maintained and even enhanced by human action.
3. To enable the students to understand how technology has made some resources more valuable than others.
4. To lead them to understand and accept as a necessity the role of the government in conservation.
5. To understand that some natural resources are renewable while others are nonrenewable and that their supply can be maintained only through wise and careful use.
6. To develop in individual children, whether they live in the country or in the city, a concern for conservation and an attitude for constant personal involvement.

7. To enable the children to use information in order to make intelligent inferences about the future after studying the uses and abuses of natural resources in the past as well as their present status.

Initiation: Start a discussion by posing the question, "What would happen if something went wrong with our local water system and we could not have water for the next five days?" With proper questioning the teacher will lead the class to the adoption of the specific objectives.

PROBLEMS AND ACTIVITIES:

Problems	*Activities*
A. What are the natural resources and in what ways does man depend on them?	1. Lead children to encyclopaedias and dictionaries to find and list on the chalkboard the natural resources needing conservation.
	2. With suggestions from the children, make a list of the natural resources available in the local community. Visit one or two.
	3. What additional resources does the community need and from what places do they come? Assign individual children to find out. Have them make a wall map of the U.S.A. and pinpoint the locations.
	4. Have children write a composition on the topic "Life without natural resources." Read to the class the most dramatic compositions.
	5. Show the film *Water Works for Us* and/or *The Story of Petroleum.*
	6. Urge children to readings

such as *Great Heritage, Water—Or Your Life* and *Wildlife for America.*

B. What have been some of the results of man's failure to protect and conserve natural resources?

1. Point out the effects of the unwise use of forests by showing the film *Forest Conservation.*
2. Assign appropriate sections from the book *First Book of Conservation.*
3. Show the film *Seeds of Destruction.*
4. Ask a child to report on the book *The Treasure of Watchdog Mountain* and continue with a discussion on the interrelation of plants, animals, man and nature's forces.
5. Show the film *Yours Is the Land* in order to emphasize the interdependence of natural resources.
6. Identify cases of misuse of natural resources in the local area and reflect with the class upon their effects.

C. What have been some of man's ways and efforts to conserve natural resources?

1. Present methods of preventing overgrazing by showing the film *Grassland.* Also, show the film *Irrigation Farming.*
2. Certain children may be stimulated to read and report on "A River Is Tamed: The Story of TVA" in *Our Wonderful World* and *Our Country's National Parks.*
3. Show the film *Life in the Central Valley of California.*
4. Children may now prepare charts showing the misuses as

D. What is the status of natural resources at the present? What resources do we value more today and why?

well as the methods of conservation of natural resources in the past.

1. Discuss the unequal distribution of natural resources around the world and its effects upon the lives of people and upon the relationships of nations. Ask the question: "What resources assume more importance due to technological developments?"

2. Use natural resources maps of the world and the U.S.A.

3. Assign "A Nation Takes Stock of Its Resources" in *Our Wonderful World*.

4. Invite the local conservation agent to come and talk to the class about the status of natural resources in the local area.

5. Alert the children to current conservation articles in the news media.

E. What role does the government play in conservation?

1. Have two groups debate the issue, "Should the Government Play a Role in Conservation?"

2. Write to the Superintendent of Documents and the U.S. Departments of Agriculture and Interior for appropriate information.

3. Show the film *Free Horizons*.

4. Have them read "The Government in Conservation."

F. What should be the individual's role in conservation?

1. Discuss fire prevention measures as well as ways in which

to preserve the beauty of the countryside and the purity of our waters.

2. Show the film *Susan and the Forest Fire.*

3. Have each child write a conservation pledge and together select the best one to be posted or even submitted for publication in the school paper or local press.

G. How does the future look in view of the fact that the population increases and the natural resources decrease?

1. This probably is a problem for high school students, but a general discussion to simply identify a basic world-wide concern will be neither out of place nor too difficult.

Culminating activity: Organize a campaign to alert the community to local conservation problems and urge every citizen to fulfill his responsibilities.

Evaluation: The children will constantly be evaluated during discussions. Their written work and other projects will be checked. The culminating activity will provide a good opportunity for children to show what they learned. The attitude of children towards conservation will be observed as much as possible in everyday life. Various kinds of pencil and paper tests may be used. Also, an attempt will be made to notice the carry-over from this unit to other subjects.

RESOURCES:

A. Bibliography:
1. Carhart, A. H., *Water—Or Your Life.* Philadelphia: J.B. Lippincott Co., 1951.
2. Evers, A., *The Treasure of Watchdog Mountain.* New York: the Macmillan Co., 1955.
3. Graham, H. E. and W. R. Van Dersal, *Wildlife for America.* New York: Oxford University Press, 1949.
4. Melbo, I. R., *Our Country's National Parks.* Indianapolis: Bobbs-Merrill, 1950.
5. Shippen, K. B., *Great Heritage.* New York: Viking Press, Inc., 1947.

6. Smith, F. C., *First Book of Conservation*. New York: Franklin Watts, Inc., 1954.
7. "A River Is Tamed: The Story of TVA," *Our Wonderful World*, Vol. 8, p. 38.
8. "The Government in Conservation," *Our Wonderful World*, Vol. 12, p. 404.

B. Films:

1. *Forest Conservation*. Encyclopaedia Britannica Films, Inc., sound motion picture, color, 11 min.
2. *Free Horizons*. Films, Inc., sound motion picture, black and white, 22 min.
3. *Grassland*. U.S. Department of Agriculture, sound motion picture, black and white, 11 min.
4. *Irrigation Farming*. Encyclopaedia Britannica Films, Inc., sound motion picture, black and white, 10 min.
5. *Life in the Central Valley of California*. Coronet Films, sound motion picture, color, 11 min.
6. *Seeds of Destruction*. Encyclopaedia Britannica Films, Inc., sound motion picture, color, 10 min.
7. *The Story of Petroleum*. Encyclopaedia Britannica Films, Inc., sound motion picture, black and white, 11 min.
8. *Water Works for Us*. Young America Films, sound motion picture, black and white, 10 min.
9. *Yours Is the Land*. Encyclopaedia Britannica Films, Inc., sound motion picture, color, 20 min.

C. Places to visit:

1. Sites of natural resources in local area.
2. Sites where natural resources were misused in the past.

D. People to invite:

1. Local conservation agent.

COMMERCIAL RESOURCE UNITS

Listed below are sources from which teachers can secure resource units with the specific titles available. All schools are urged to purchase these titles and make them available to their teachers. The teachers, in turn, are urged to use them wisely in developing their own units.

A. F. A. Owen Publishing Co., Dansville, N. Y., publishes two portfolios with resource units in the following topics: American Citizenship, Character Education, Christmas Customs, City Life, Colonial Life,

Community Life, Exploring the World, Family Life, Farm Life, History of Democracy, Living in a Democracy, Money and Banking, The Nation's Health, Old World Gifts, Our Democracy, Our Schools, Post Office, Safety Education, Shelter, Thanksgiving, United Nations, Africa, Alaska, Australia, Canada, Early Indians, Eskimos, Holland, India and Pakistan, Indians, Japan, Mexico, Middle Ages, Middle West, New England, Pacific States, Pioneer Life, Rocky Mountain States, South America (two), Switzerland.

B. *The World Book Encyclopedia, Field Enterprises Educational Corporation, Merchandise Mart Plaza, Chicago, Illinois 60654,* publishes the following resource units: American Indians, American Industrialization, Argentina, Brazil, Climate, Colonial Life in America, Communication, Conservation, Europe, Farming, Federal Government of the United States, Food, Homes, Latin America, Pioneer Life, Post Office, Transportation, United Nations, Westward Movement.

C. *The Educational Division of F. E. Compton Co., Division of Encyclopaedia Britannica, Inc., 1000 N. Dearborn Street, Chicago, Illinois 60610,* publishes the following teaching guides or reference outlines just as helpful as the resource units: American Heritage, Studying the State, East Asia, Africa, Canada, Ancient History, Australia and New Zealand, Austria and Austria-Hungary, China, Citizenship, Clothing, Communication, Conservation, Denmark and Iceland, Economics, Education, Europe, Food, France, Geography, Germany, Great Britain and Ireland, India, Individual Freedom, Industrial Revolution, American Industry, Italy, Japan, Mexico, Middle Ages, Netherlands and Belgium, North America, Races of Mankind, Renaissance and Reformation, Russia, Shelter and Housing, South America, Spain and Portugal, Sweden and Norway, Switzerland, Transportation, United States.

D. Also, *Encyclopaedia Britannica, Inc., 20 N. Wacker Dr., Chicago Illinois,* publishes the following Britannica Junior Study Guides: The American Indian, The Eskimo, Mexico, Netherlands, China and Japan, Cold Lands and Hot Lands, Discovery and Exploration, Transportation, Unites States History, Central America and South America.

E. *C. A. Gregory Co., 345 Calhoun Street, Cincinnati 1, Ohio,* publishes resource unit materials developed by the Citizenship Education Project of Teachers College, Columbia University. These materials are junior and senior high school oriented, but could be very useful to the elementary schools as well. They include the following topics: Courts, Elections, Government, International Relations, Legislation, Community Agencies, Community Development, Community Structure, Consumer Information, Disaster, Preparedness, Economic System, Education, Employment, Housing, National Emergency, Recreation, School Improvement, Communication Media, Family, Intercultural Relations, Old Age, Personal Behavior, Public Opinion—Propaganda, Conservation, Public Health, Safety, Technology, Transportation.

F. Wilhelmina Hill, *Selected Resource Units.* Curriculum Series Number Eleven. (Washington, D. C.: National Council for the Social Studies, National Education Association, 1961). This is a collection of 21 units for grades K—6.

G. Ernest W. Tiegs and Fay Adams, *Teaching the Social Studies.* (New York: Ginn and Company, 1958). The following three units are included in the appendix: Home and Community, People Who Found Our Country, and Mexico.

H. Lavone A. Hanna *et al. Unit Teaching in the Elementary School.* (New York: Holt, Rinehart and Winston, 1963). pp. 449–574. The following resource units are developed: Living in Japan, How the Pioneers Moved Westward, How Air Transportation Affects Social Living, and Great Britain.

I. John U. Michaelis, *Social Studies for Children in a Democracy.* Second Edition. (Englewood Cliffs, N. J.: Prentice-Hall, 1956). The following two units are included in the appendix: The Farm and Early American Life.

J. John U. Michaelis, ed. *Teaching Units in the Social Sciences* (Chicago: Rand McNally and Company, 1966). There are three volumes for the elementary grades containing recently developed units which are based on the social sciences.

K. Ralph C. Preston, *Teaching Social Studies in the Elementary School.* Revised edition. (New York: Holt, Rinehart and Winston, 1962). pp. 100–250. In these pages Dr. Preston briefly deals with the following categories of units: units emphasizing the community, units emphasizing social processes, units emphasizing regions and cultures, and units emphasizing the past.

B. The lesson plan

The lesson plan is a subdivision of the unit plan; it lasts only one period while the unit runs into several days or even weeks. The unit plan is in essence a series of lesson plans.

The basic elements of the structure of the lesson plan are again the objectives, the content and its presentation, and the techniques of evaluation. As far as the objectives are concerned and the ways they are determined, the same guidelines described for the unit apply. The objectives should not be simply pages to be covered or exercises to be done. They should be the understanding of verbalized relationships of broad applicability capable of modifying the behavior of the children in terms of their ability to make intelligent decisions and increase their capacity for learning. Also, the objectives of the lesson plan should be directed toward the development of desirable attitudes and the acquisition of certain social skills. The objectives of each lesson plan are not different from the objectives of the unit which the lesson represents. They are the same but fewer in number in each lesson.

In the unit the content and its presentation was referred to as the problems and activities. The term used to identify this structural part in the lesson plan is procedure. One thing which should be emphasized here is that the procedure should not be an outline of the content to be covered. Instead, it should be everything the teacher plans to do with the class in order to convey the content to the children and reach the objectives. She might use maps to identify a relationship, she might have a planning session, she might have the children report on research which they conducted or she might undertake with them any other type of activity.

If a teacher develops a unit the way it is suggested in this chapter, the lesson plans for that particular unit will already be prepared to a great extent. The objectives are all identified and stated. One or two content problems and the related activities will constitute the procedure. The evaluation techniques are also spelled out in general terms and the concern in the development of the lesson plan should be how to implement them in detail.

Available forms on lesson plans include other structural elements besides the objectives, the procedure and the techniques of evaluation. Initiation and follow-up activities are occasionally identified separately instead of being placed as the first and last activities in the procedure. Materials to be used, even the blackboard, are sometimes described in more detail than it is necessary. Objectives are often stated in all kinds of "hair-splitting" subcategories. The differences between these subcategories are so fine that even the best teachers have difficulty distinguishing them. The suggestion is made here to eliminate all structural elements of secondary nature and concentrate on the objectives, the procedure, and the techniques of evaluation. Realistically, teachers are too busy to make lesson plans with other than the necessary structural elements included. As a matter of fact, crowding the lesson plans with the various structural elements of secondary nature is a sure way of discouraging the teachers to prepare lesson plans.

As far as the evaluation techniques of lesson plans are concerned, whatever was said in connection with the evaluation of the unit applies here as well. The teacher should always be alert to make sure the children are learning whatever is being taught to them.

Summary

Unit teaching, considering the nature of social studies and modern theories of learning, appears to be the best method of teaching social studies. It is, however, more difficult than textbook teaching. To suggest that teachers abandon the textbook immediately and move into unit teaching is impractical. An approach is needed on the basis of which the teachers will move slowly from one type of teaching to the other. Of course, the teachers should understand first the merits of unit teaching.

The main structural elements of the unit are the objectives (general and specific), the problems and activities and the evaluation techniques. An initiation activity to arouse the interest of the children to the study of the unit is recommended. Also, culminating activities to summarize for all the children the outcomes of the unit are necessary. The last section in writing a unit is the listing of all resources to be used.

The lesson plan is similar to the unit plan as far as structure is concerned. It has objectives, procedure (the equivalent of problems and activities in the unit), and techniques of evaluation. A lesson plan is a strategy for a shorter period of time and is a part of the broader strategy which is the unit.

Providing Effective Resources:
Reading Materials and
Community Resources

6

Providing Effective Resources:
Reading Materials and
Community Resources

The method of teaching social studies recommended throughout this book is the inquiry approach in the development of concepts and generalizations commonly referred to as "big ideas." These big ideas supply the specific objectives for unit and lesson plans and, as was shown in the preceding chapter, suggest specific content problems or logical questions to be answered by the children through planned and directed activities.

In order for this method to succeed, the teacher and the children must use a variety of materials coming from resources available. This chapter deals with two of the resources, reading materials other than textbooks and resources which can be found in and around the local community.

A. Reading materials

In talking about reading materials, the teacher in the elementary school should be concerned with three basic questions:

114

1. What skills do the children need to develop in order to be able to benefit from reading?
2. What is the most effective way to utilize reading materials?
3. What reading materials are available and how can the teacher locate them?

SOCIAL STUDIES READING SKILLS

Probably the term social studies reading skills is not an appropriate one because most of the reading skills needed to understand written social studies materials are no different from the reading skills needed to understand any other written communication. The case here is one of emphasis in view of the fact that research has established that reading ability and achievement in social studies are highly correlated. On the other hand, some reading skills must be emphasized because there is less axiomatic material found in social studies than in the other content areas such as science. Since social studies deals mostly with conflicts, authors and groups unavoidably tend to color their writings with their own opinions, views, and biases. The child should be able to evaluate reading materials and detect these negative elements.

Reading skills needed in social studies could be classified in three major categories: (1) Locating reading information; (2) understanding reading information; and (3) critically evaluating reading information.

Locating reading information. Under this category the following skills could be included:

1. The use of the table of contents.
2. The use of the index of a book.
3. Skimming to formulate a general idea about the content of a written communication or for the purpose of locating specific information.
4. The use of the library in terms of knowing what the holdings of a library are and being able to use the card catalogue as well as the various periodical indices.
5. The ability to take notes.

The use of the table of contents and indices are simple skills which require practice in a functional context. Children will develop these skills through involvement in learning situations in which the table of contents and the index are used. Like all skills, they do not develop through lecturing about them. Quite often we find teachers explaining the table of contents in the first grade by making a book of the experience charts to which they attach a table with all the titles of the charts.

Practice in the use of the table of contents and the indices introduces the children to the skill of skimming. In skimming, besides the table of contents and the index, the reader is aided by subheadings, pictures, illustrations, maps, tables, graphs, diagrams, and charts. In some books or other written communications summaries are provided which can be helpful in giving a general overview.

Skimming is a skill helpful to children in developing their ability to make inferences on the basis of a few clues. It is a rather difficult skill and children should be closely guided in its development. One particular teacher had the children practice skimming by playing a guessing game. She gave the children a book and asked them to suggest clues in regard to the content of the book by skimming through. She wrote these clues on the blackboard. The children were then asked to guess what the book was all about on the basis of these clues. After all guesses were recorded, the children were asked to read the book and decide which guess was most correct.

Another important skill in locating information is the ability to use the library. Schools all over the world have recognized the value of the school library, but only here in the United States was it financially possible to have so many of them. If there are some schools which do not have libraries, it is probably due to the lack of enthusiasm on the part of the teachers. Teachers who recognize the value of a school library can exercise enough pressure to get one.

The development of the skill to use the library requires first the development of a thirst for books. This thirst and enthusiasm for books often is transferred from the teacher to the children. Only if the teacher uses a variety of reading resources which are available in the library, will the children see the value of the library. In planning a unit or a lesson, the teacher should have read much of the related reading materials that are available locally. Only then will she be able to successfully direct the children to reading beyond the textbook.

Some teachers, in an effort to be progressive, have the children write reports on various topics, but they do not give them directions in terms of resources. The children then copy out of the only encyclopedia which happens to be available statements which they do not understand. The teacher should know not only the holdings on various topics, but the level of difficulty of each book as well. This will enable her to make the appropriate distribution of the reading materials.

In the beginning stages, teachers should not send the children to the library to find materials on their own. Not knowing the process, they might get frustrated and give up forever. Whenever children need materials, take them by the hand and go through the whole process together. Make sure the use of the library is taught within the context of problem solving situations. Never make it an academic exercise.

The library should always be open and the children should be able to go to it for materials whenever they need them. Opening the library a few hours a week and scheduling classes in the library are contradictory to the functions of the library.

Finally, the last skill in locating information is the ability to take notes in order to easily relocate information. Unless reading is done for pleasure, information gained through it is usually put to some kind of use later. Notes are necessary to avoid going through the elaborate process of relocating it. There are some pitfalls which should be avoided in note-taking. Some people tend to take too many notes while others do not take enough. The first thing to remember is the purpose for which the reading is done. If reading is done to locate specific information, there is no need for the child to take notes on anything other than that specific information. When the child is interested in an entire written communication, he must note down all basic structural elements of that communication. In order for the child to do this he must be able to discover the main and subordinate ideas of the author. More about this is presented in the following section.

Understanding reading information. Under this category the following skills could be included:

1. Skills for attacking new words.
2. Discovering the organization of ideas.
3. Being able to see relationships.
4. Being able to make inferences.

Many of the concepts involved in social studies are intangible and, therefore, difficult. Knowledge of the meaning of one of these concepts could, in many cases, be the key to the understanding of a whole passage. It is imperative, therefore, that the children know how to attack new words through clues, context and other means. Here is an area where the teacher could correlate reading and social studies.

Another skill in the understanding of reading information is the ability to discover the structure of ideas used by the author. The children should get practice in identifying the overall theme of the book, the main idea and the subordinate ideas in each section, chapter and paragraph. By developing this skill, the children will be capable of reducing a written communication to a skeletal outline.

Discovering the structure of reading information leads to another important skill, the ability to see relationships. When a child reads a book about a boat and is capable of describing the bridge and the engine room in detail he has not gone very far. The important thing for the child is to see the relationship between the engine room and the bridge. When children begin to talk for the first time, "why" is always on the tip of their tongues. What happens to them when they reach school? Teachers should encourage the children to continue asking "why" and provide situations in which this will be possible.

One kind of relationship which the children should be capable of discovering is cause and effect. Drought in Kansas causes reduced grain production. What does it mean when we read in the papers that India had a drought? Seeing cause and effect relationships enables the youngsters to use their minds in making inferences.

Critical evaluation of reading information. Under this category the following skills could be included:

1. The ability to distinguish between fact and opinion.
2. The ability to recognize propaganda material.
3. The ability to discover contradictions and examine the reasons for them.
4. The ability to detect the biases of the authors.

It used to be that whatever was put in print was considered the final word. This is no longer so and the children should realize it. The realization of this fact is very important because it constitutes the basis for reading critically.

The most practical level to start teaching about the difference between fact and opinion is the local newspaper. Point out the differences between the reports on actual happenings and the views expressed on the editorial page. Bring illustrations to show that almost everyone agrees on the facts, while an opinion may be held by only one individual. Children should understand that opinions must be intelligent statements based on some facts. Also, children should develop a positive attitude towards opinions and they should be encouraged to express their own opinion on various issues. Courage and ability to express one's opinion develop the ability to formulate hypotheses.

Another skill to be developed in children is the ability to recognize propaganda. There is a tendency to think of all propaganda as distortion. This is not necessarily true. The intent of propaganda is to convince. There is nothing wrong about this as long as reality is not distorted in the process. When the truth is twisted in an effort to convince one about something, propaganda becomes bad.

Unfortunately, there is much bad propaganda that reaches the children and they should be protected from it. Evaluating reading materials on the basis of sound criteria and comparing their content with authentic resources is a demanding intellectual activity.

The ability of the children to read critically will further be developed by making them sensitive to contradictions within a written communication or between two or more of them on the same subject. There may be a variety of reasons for the existence of contradictions, but the most common is probably the author's bias. Children should be directed in evaluating the qualifications and the motives of the author of any written communication.

The skills necessary to read critically do not develop overnight. Neither will they be fully developed by the time the children leave the elementary school. A conscious effort to develop them should be made, however, as early as possible. The children's understanding of their social environment and their self-development depends to a great extent on what they read and how they read it.

METHOD OF UTILIZING READING MATERIALS

The method of utilizing reading materials is dictated by the method of teaching advocated throughout this book. In form of a summary, this method of teaching consists of the following steps:

1. The teacher selects a basic theme that will pervade the year's work.
2. She identifies the concepts and/or generalizations to be taught.
3. She interprets the concepts and generalizations to specific behaviors to be developed in children.
4. She sets up a number of content problems the solution of which will lead to the realization of the objectives.
5. The teacher and the children plan a variety of activities, or learning experiences, through which the children will find solutions to the problems.

The unit method, as explained in chapter 5, reflects the steps outlined above. The title of the unit is related to the general theme adapted for the grade. The objectives are the concepts and generalizations or the specific behaviors to which concepts and generalizations have been reduced. The problems result from the conversion of the content which is related to the topic into a number of basic questions. As a final step in preparing a unit, the teacher designs the learning activities.

Directing the youngsters to various reading materials provides them with one type of learning activity. Teachers use reading materials in order to serve a variety of functions. The following are some of these functions:

1. To motivate the children towards the study of a topic. Many teachers have a display area in which they display books before undertaking the study of a topic. The children become interested in these books, browse through them and are stimulated to raise questions.
2. To find specific information such as dates, names, locations.
3. To collect information to write a report or to prepare a skit.
4. To obtain a variety of points of view on an issue.
5. To analyze a specific written communication.

When the teacher assigns reading materials she should keep in mind a number of basic guidelines:

1. She should always remember that the children read with differing ability. She should have available reading materials representing a wide range of levels of difficulty.
2. Some children can benefit more from picture books and books with colorful illustrations.

3. The teacher should check the load of new words and help the children with the most difficult ones.
4. The objectives for children with wide individual differences do not have to vary though the materials do.

WHERE AND HOW TO OBTAIN READING MATERIALS

There is a vast amount of reading materials available. Many of these materials have to be purchased while others reach the classroom without even asking for them. In both cases the teacher has to make choices in order to meet budgetary limitations and the abilities of children and in order to eliminate propaganda materials with no educational value. To help the teacher in locating and selecting reading materials, a number of references, sources, and books are suggested in this section. The value of all these sources has been demonstrated because everything included in the lists below is the most recent and most useful material from the shelves of an excellent school library.

Encyclopedias:

1. *Britannica Junior Encyclopaedia.* Chicago: Encyclopaedia Britannica, Inc. The purpose of the editors is to provide an interesting, easy-to-use, and easily understood reference source for the elementary school child. Topics are arranged alphabetically with cross reference provided.
2. *Childcraft.* Chicago: Field Enterprises Educational Corporation. The contents were selected on the basis of the known curiosities and interests of young children. Each volume deals with one broad area such as "Holidays and Customs," "Places to Know" and others.
3. *Compton's Pictured Encyclopedia and Fact Index.* Chicago: F. E. Compton Co. Good for children and young people. Topics are alphabetically arranged. Yearly supplements are provided.
4. *Lands and People.* New York: Grolier, Inc. A seven volume set dealing with man's earthly environment and his relations with it. Each volume deals with one area of the world. It is well illustrated.
5. *Our Wonderful World.* Chicago: Spencer Press, Inc. An 18 volume set containing articles and stories designed to meet children's real and expressed interests. Stories on a particular

topic are spread throughout all of the volumes so that the whole class can deal with the same topic at once.

6. *Pictorial Encyclopedia of American History*. Chicago: Children's Press, Inc. An excellent source for the young child and especially the slow reader and the slow learner. Volumes are chronologically arranged.

7. *The New Golden Encyclopedia*. New York: Golden Press. One volume with topics alphabetically arranged. A child's treasury of information about our world illustrated in full color.

8. *The World Book Encyclopedia*. Chicago: Field Enterprises Educational Corporation. Good for children in all grades. Topics are alphabetically arranged. Yearly supplements provided. Also available in a Large Type Edition.

9. *Worldmark Encyclopedia of the Nations*. New York: Worldmark Press, Inc. Each volume is devoted to one major part of the world and gives vital information country by country.

10. *Young People's Story of Our Heritage*. Chicago: Children's Press. A set of 14 volumes intended to project the young reader into the mainstream of creative thought and effort that characterized the progress of our civilization. It is well illustrated.

Yearbooks and Dictionaries:

1. *A Dictionary of the Social Sciences*. Compiled under the auspices of the United Nations Educational, Scientific, and Cultural Organization and edited by Julius Gould and William L. Kolb. New York: The Free Press, 1964.

2. *Chamber's Biographical Dictionary*. New York: St. Martin's Press, Inc., 1962. One volume edition with over 15,000 biographies.

3. *Current Biography Yearbook*. New York: The H. W. Wilson Co. An annual dictionary of contemporary biography which seeks to provide the reader with brief, objective, accurate, and well-documented biographical articles about living leaders in all fields of human accomplishment the world over.

4. *Information Please Almanac—Atlas and Yeabook*. New York: Simon-Schuster. Published annually.

5. *Scott's Standard Postage Stamp Catalogue*. New York: Scott Publications. Published annually.

6. *The Life Treasury of American Folklore*. New York: Time, Inc., 1961.

7. *The World Almanac and Book of Facts*. New York: New York World-Telegram. Published annually.

Sources of Trade Books:

1. Alm, Richard S., ed., *Books for You*. New York: Washington Square Press, Inc., 1964.
2. Arbuthnot, May Hill, *Children and Books*. New York: Scott, Foresman, 1957.
3. Arbuthnot, May Hill and others, *Children's Books Too Good to Miss*. Cleveland: Western Reserve University Press, 1948.
4. *Bibliography of Books for Children*. Washington, D. C.: Association for Childhood Education International, 1965.
5. *Catalog of Large Type Materials*. 3901 Balboa Street, San Francisco: National Aid to Visual Handicapped, 1964. The books suggested are also good for slow readers.
6. *Children's Catalog*, 10th ed. New York: H. W. Wilson Co., 1961. Yearly supplements provided.
7. Davis, John E., "A List of Bibliographies to Serve the Classroom Teacher as Guides to the Selection of Literature for Enrichment of the Social Studies," *Curriculum Bulletin* of the School of Education of the University of Oregon, December 1962.
8. Eakin, Mary K., "Library Materials for Holidays," *Instructional Materials Bulletin* of Iowa State Teachers College Library, May 1962.
9. *Famous Americans for Young Americans*. Albany: The New York State Education Department, 1966.
10. Hunt, Mate Graye, *Values Resource Guide*. Oneonta, N.Y.: American Association of Colleges for Teacher Education, 1958.
11. Huus, Helen, *Children's Books to Enrich the Social Studies*. Washington, D.C.: The National Council for the Social Studies, 1961. Contains 618 selected titles arranged according to topics. All selections are annotated and grade level suggested.
12. Johnson, Edna, and others, *Anthology of Children's Literature*. Boston: Houghton Mifflin, 1959.
13. Larrick, Nancy, *A Teacher's Guide to Children's Books*. Columbus, Ohio: Charles E. Merrill Books, Inc., 1960.
14. Mathes, Miriam Snow, *A Basic Book Collection for Elementary Grades*. Chicago: American Library Association, 1960.

15. *Reference Materials for School Libraries.* Publication No. 385. Raleigh, N.C.: North Carolina Department of Public Instruction, 1965.
16. Rue, Eloise, *Subject Index to Books for Intermediate Grades.* Chicago: American Library Association, 1950.
17. *Social Studies Bibliography—Elementary School.* Albany: The New York State Education Department, 1960.
18. Tooze, Ruth, *Your Children Want to Read, A Guide for Teachers and Parents.* Englewood Cliffs, N.J.: Prentice-Hall, Inc., 1957.
19. Tooze, Ruth and Krone, B. P., *Literature and Music as Resources for Social Studies.* Englewood Cliffs, N.J.: Prentice-Hall, Inc., 1955.

Sources for Free and Inexpensive Materials:

1. *Better Living Booklets,* Chicago: Science Research Associates. Series of booklets on various topics written by authorities for various age groups.
2. *Catalog of Free Teaching Aids.* Box 943, Riverside, California: Gordon Salisbury and Robert Sheridan.
3. *Educator's Index to Free Materials.* Randolph, Wisc.: Educators Progress Service.
4. *Elementary Teachers Guide to Free Curriculum Materials.* Randolph, Wisc.: Educators Progress Service. It is published yearly and describes about 1,200 free materials.
5. *Free and Inexpensive Learning Materials.* Nashville: George Peabody College for Teachers.
6. *Pamphleteer Monthly.* New York: Pamphleteer Distributions Co.
7. *Representative Government Best Sellers.* Washington, D.C.: U.S. Government Printing Office.
8. *Sources of Free and Inexpensive Teaching Aids.* Box 369, Riverside, Calif.: Bruce Miller.
9. *Sources of Free and Inexpensive Educational Materials.* Chicago: Field Enterprises, Inc.
10. *The Pamphlet Index.* 119 West 23rd Street, New York, N.Y.
11. *Vertical File Index.* New York: The H. W. Wilson Co.

Magazines and Newspapers:

All adult magazines such as *Life, Look,* and *National Geographic* and most of the adult newspapers are very useful. Also, there are several graded children's magazines and newspapers. These are listed in chapter 8 in connection with the treatment of "Current Events."

Suggested Trade Books:

A large book exhibit was planned in one of the laboratory schools in New York State. The children from all grades were allowed to browse through the books and suggest the titles which they wished to have in their school library. Following are some of the suggested titles which are related to social studies. For purposes of saving space, only the author, the title of the book, and the recommended age level are given. If the content of the book cannot be easily inferred from the title, it is suggested in parentheses. The books were classified by the librarian as follows:

PICTURE AND EASY BOOKS:

1. Joslin, S. *There Is a Bull in My Balcony.* 6 and up. (Mexico)
2. Jupo, F. *Count Carrot.* 6–9. (German folktale)
3. Kessler, L. *Mrs. Pine Takes a Trip.* 5–8. (All about housework)
4. Lindgren, A. *Springtime in Noisy Village.* 5–9.
5. Rey, M. *Curious George Goes to the Hospital.* 6–7.
6. Schwortz, J. *Go on Wheels,* 6–9.

INTERMEDIATE BOOKS:

1. Freschet, B. *Kangaroo Red.* 6–10. (Australia)
2. Fry, R. *The Castle Family.* 8–12. (family life)
3. Hicks, C. *Alvin Fernald, Foreign Trader.* 8–11.
4. Morgan, B. *Journey for Tobiyah.* 9–12. (Jewish History)
5. Stephens, P. *Towappu.* 9–12. (Indians)
6. Stolz, M. *Maximilian's World.* 6–10. (Mexico)

MYSTERIES AND TALL TALES:

1. Adrian M. *The Indian Horse Mystery.* 8–13. (Indian life)
2. Clark, M. C. *Adirondack Mountain Mystery.* 10 and up.
3. Pallas, N. *The S. S. Shamrock Mystery.* 11–15. (travel in Great Lakes)
4. Thompson, D. *Loon Lake Mystery.* 10–14. (life in Alaska)
5. DeLage, I. *The Farmer and the Witch.* 8–11.

SOCIAL SCIENCES:

1. Bweher, I. *Sea Monsters.* 8–12.
2. Carlson, C. *Water Fit to Use.* 10–15.

3. Faber, D. *Captive Rivers: The Story of Big Dams*. 10–14.
4. Hanff, H. *Good Neighbors: The Peace Corps in Latin America*. 8–12.
5. Hanff, H. *Religious Freedom: The American Story*. 8–12.
6. Weisgard, L. *Life Long Ago: First Farmer*. 11 and up.

FAIRY TALES AND FOLKLORE:

1. Brown, M. *Backbone of the King*. 10–14. (Hawaiian legend)
2. Buck, P. *Fairy Tales of the Orient*. 10 and up.
3. Haviland, V. *Favorite Fairy Tales Told in Czechoslovakia*. 7–11.
4. Larson, J. *Palace in Bagdad*. 8–12. (Seven tales from the Middle East)
5. Serrallier, I. *A Fall from the Sky: The Story of Daedalus*. 8–12. (Mythology—Aviation)
6. Stoutenburg, A. *American Tall Tales*. 9–12.
7. Thompson, V. *Hawaiian Myths of Earth, Sea, and Sky*. 8–12.

HOLIDAY BOOKS:

1. Phelan, M. *The Fourth of July*. 7–10.
2. Cone, M. *The Jewish Sabbath*. 7–10.
3. Bulla, C. *Lincoln's Birthday*. 7–10.

HISTORY AND GEOGRAPHY:

1. Buehr, W. *Portuguese Explorers*. 8–12.
2. Burt, O. *Old America Comes Alive*. 9–12.
3. Coldwell, J. *Let's Visit Vietnam*. 9–12.
4. Carse, R. *The High Country*. 10–14. (exploration of Canada)
5. Hodges, C. *The Norman Conquest*. 8–12.
6. Palmer, G. *Quest for Prehistory*. 11–15.
7. Sasek, M. *This is Greece*. 8 and up.
8. Spencer, C. *China's Leaders in Ideas and Action*. 10 and up. (from Confucius to Chou En-Lai)

LIVING IN TODAY'S WORLD

1. Watson, J. *India: Old Land, New Nation*. 9–13.
2. Watson, J. *Iran: Crossroad of Caravans*. 9–13.

IN AMERICA BOOKS:

1. Cates, E. *The English in America*. 11–16.
2. Kunz, V. *The French in America*. 11–16.
3. Lass, W. *The Germans in America*. 11–16.
4. Johnson, J. *The Irish in America*, 11–16.

5. Grossman, R. *The Italians in America.* 11–16.
6. Spangler, E. *The Negro in America.* 11–16.
7. Johnson, J. *The Scotch in America.* 11–16.
8. Hillbrand, P. *The Swedes in America.* 11–16.

LET'S TRAVEL BOOKS:

1. Geis, D. *Congo.* 11 and up.
2. Geis, D. *Philippines.* 11 and up.
3. Geis, D. *Thailand.* 11 and up.

BIOGRAPHIES:

1. Newman, S. *Marion Anderson: Lady from Philadelphia.* 10–16.
2. Severn, B. *In Lincoln's Footsteps: The Life of Andrew Johnson.* 11 and up.
3. Syme, R. *William Penn, Founder of Pennsylvania.* 10 and up.
4. Graves, C. *Eleanor Roosevelt.* 8–11.
5. Blassingame, W. *Franklin D. Roosevelt.* 8–11.
6. Henry, J. *Andrew Carnegie.* 8–11.
7. Dareff, H. *Jacqueline Kennedy: A Portrait in Courage.* 10–17.

There is no doubt that the reading materials suggested thus far and their proper utilization will contribute towards a rich social studies program. Some, however, might say that they cost too much. In this affluent country the money obstacle has always been overcome and it can be overcome in this case, also. When the teacher is enthusiastic about what she is doing and uses the material, the administration will give in. All reading materials do not have to be purchased at one time. A few each year will eventually lead to a good collection. Teachers should not forget that many of the materials can be had either free or for very little money. Besides, the federal government has been recently allocating considerable amounts of money for the enrichment of school libraries.

B. Community resources

It was pointed out in the third chapter that the local community provides the best laboratory for the teaching of social science concepts and generalizations. In the conventional social studies programs the primary grades have always dealt with the community. Though the new programs use a different approach, they still recommend the study of the community as the most appropriate for the primary grades. This does not mean, however, that community resources cannot be useful in the upper grades. There are people, things, and real situations in the community which can assist in the development of concepts and generalizations at any level. In order to encourage the teachers to effectively use the community in designing learning activities, this section deals with the following:

1. Research evidence is presented showing that teachers do not use community resources as much as they should.
2. The need is stressed for the teacher to have a thorough knowledge of the community, and suggestions are provided for acquiring such knowledge.
3. A list is provided of community resources in order to show their wide variety and to stimulate teachers to locate the resources in their own community.
4. Some illustrations are offered to show how community resources have been successfully used to enrich the social studies.

COMMUNITY RESOURCES OUGHT TO BE UTILIZED MORE

A research study, the most recent of its kind, was undertaken in Detroit by Miller Collings[1] in order to determine how much direct experience with the community the pupils were receiving. A questionnaire was devised which listed 67 opportunities by which children could acquire direct experience in and around Detroit. Included in this list were such items as cultural facilities, communication, recreation, transportation, commercial, and industrial agencies.

The results indicated that pupils have had some direct experiences with some places, but many educational opportunities in existence right within the community were neglected. Most boys and girls who had visited places of interest in the community had done so with parents and friends and not with a school group. It is interesting to note that more than 90 percent of the twelfth graders questioned had never visited such civic functions as a City Council meeting, a Fire Department Training School, a Garbage Disposal system, or the Water Works. Students had most of their direct experiences with recreational and cultural activities, and fewest experiences with government activities.

---

[1] Miller R. Collings, "Exploring Your Community: A Direct Experience Study." *The Journal of Educational Research*. Volume 44 (November 1950), pp. 225–230.

The Collings study was reviewed here not so much for the value of the results as such, but as a motivating factor to make the teachers review their situation and determine whether they make full use of the educational opportunities in their own communities. There seems to be no doubt that the utilization of the community resources enriches the social studies program and brings about better results. As early as 1943 Ella Callista Clark[2] supported this claim with a study which was to determine what contributions excursions to the local Institute of Arts, the plant of the local paper, the telephone company, and the local transportation facilities might yield in four sixth-grade units on Egypt, Printing, Transportation, and Communication. She concluded that a carefully designed excursion has the power to develop interests, ideals, and appreciations in children along with increasing their knowledge.

GET TO KNOW THE COMMUNITY

In order for the teacher to be able to make a better utilization of the community she must know what resources are in the community. Many of our teachers do not reside in the community in which they teach. In the big cities, and especially in the deprived neighborhoods, many of the teachers make every effort to ignore and forget the conditions in which the children exist and the values which motivate their behavior. Their teaching is based on a context different from the one in which the children live and for this reason is in many cases unsucessful.

All teachers, the commuters and the residents, those who identify with the social environment of the children and those who do not, must get to know thoroughly the community in which they teach. Every teacher must make a community survey in order to answer the following questions:

1. What are the people like in this community in terms of their occupations, their interests, their recreations, their attitudes, their cultural and historical backgrounds, their civic mindedness, their conflicts and problems?

2. What is the nature of the basic social functions in the com-

---

[2] Ella C. Clark, "An Experimental Evaluation of the School Excursion," *Journal of Experimental Education.* Volume 12 (September 1943), pp. 10–19.

munity such as government, recreation, transportation, communication, religious expression, food production and supply, attitude towards and provisions for health?

3. What is the history of the community, its important geographic features, and its industries?

There are formal techniques for surveying the community such as interview, observation and documentary analysis. A teacher may learn much about the community by taking walks around the town, eating in the restaurants, and riding the buses. She should attend business and social gatherings, scout meetings and even various church services and functions. She should visit the local library and museums and find out about their services to the community. Also a teacher may get valuable information and materials by visiting the Chamber of Commerce and having interviews with various personalities in the community. A good way to obtain a general idea about the community neighborhoods and the houses from which the children come is to ride the school bus.

Types of Community Resources

In order to assist individual teachers, some school systems make a thorough survey of the community and file a list of all community recources in the library for every teacher's reference. One particular elementary school in the Buffalo area made use of the following resources during one year:

Kindergarten:	1. walks around school
	2. Buffalo Zoo at Delaware Park
First Grade:	3. Post Office
	4. Eggertsville Fire Station
	5. Eggertsville-Snyder Library
Second Grade:	6. Railroad Station—New York Central
	7. Bus Station—Greyhound Terminal
	8. Airport—United Airlines
	9. Buffalo Harbor
	10. Loblaw's Bakery
	11. Fairmont Foods (Dairy plant)
	12. Science Museum
	13. Federal Meat Market

Third Grade: 14. Science Museum
              15. Pheasant Hatchery
Fourth Grade: 16. Historical Museum
              17. South Park Conservatory
Fifth Grade: 18. Old Fort Niagara—Youngstown, N.Y.
              19. Fort George—Canada
              20. Fort Erie—Canada
              21. Niagara Power Project
              22. A two-hour narrated cruise of Buffalo harbor, river, Black Rock lock, and Black Rock canal.
              23. Science and Historical Museums for aspects related to curriculum.
Sixth Grade: 24. Buffalo Evening News
              25. Corning Glass Center
              26. Albright Art Gallery
              27. Science and Historical Museums for aspects related to curriculum.

Besides the places which can be visited, there are many resources which can be brought into the classroom. Such resources may include:

1. old records
2. discarded machines in attics such as spinning and carding machines
3. samples of pioneer utensils
4. types of soil and various minerals
5. scientists and inventors
6. artists, writers, and musicians
7. people with hobbies and special interests
8. old-timers
9. foreign visitors and world travelers
10. government officials, and service people

Illustration on How to Use Community Resources

There are many ways in which teachers can use the community. One third-grade teacher was trying to develop in children the concept of interdependence. In connection with this task she took the children to the nearest supermarket and had them examine packaged food in terms of origin. When they returned to the classroom, they put a world map in front of them and pulled red color strings from their town to the locations from which food originated. By looking at that map, the children could clearly see how dependent their local community was upon the rest of the world.

In order to complete the picture, the children contacted the local industry to find out the places to which their products were shipped. Then, they pulled yellow color strings from their community to these places. In this way, the children could also see how the rest of the world was dependent upon their own local community.

A sixth-grade class was attempting to determine the extent to which the various cultures around the world have been diffused and the ways in which the diffusion has taken place. In order to make this undertaking more realistic, the teacher directed the children to make a survey to find out how many musical recordings from other cultures were in the collections of the local people. Also, the children collected and exhibited all kinds of artifacts from other cultures.

Another teacher was trying to teach the generalization, "Human beings, regardless of their social and ethnic background, are nearly all capable of making contributions to culture." In order to provide realistic situations, she had the youngsters identify the various ethnic and social groups in the local community. Then, she asked the children to single out individuals from these groups who are making or have made worthwhile contributions to the life of the community and our culture in general.

Summary

There is a vast amount of reading materials available for the enrichment of social studies. In order for the youngsters to be able to benefit from reading, certain related skills must be developed. These skills would help the children to locate information, understand it and evaluate it.

Teachers or schools must have available source books in which trade books on various topics can be located. Also, teachers ought to be familiar with the various types of children's encyclopedias. There are many free and inexpensive materials useful to the teachers. The guides to these materials should always be in the teacher's hands. The various source books, encyclopedias, and guides to free and inexpensive materials are listed in this chapter along with a number of titles of trade books selected by children.

The community is another rich resource for social studies. The people, their relationships, the institutions, and the geographical features of the area provide valuable illustrations for the clarification and presentation of various concepts and generalizations of a social nature. The teacher is urged to get to know the community in which she teaches, and methods are suggested how this can be done.

Using Maps, Globes and Other Audio-Visual Aids

7

Using Maps, Globes and Other Audio-Visual Aids

Reading materials and community resources constitute two important contributions to enriching the teaching of social studies, but there is another important one. Social studies has always been associated with maps and globes. There are skills which the youngsters must develop in order to be able to use maps and globes, and there are ideas and facts which can best be understood through the use of maps and globes. A fourth major resource in making the teaching of social studies more realistic and fruitful is other audio-visual aids. This chapter is devoted to the treatment of these two categories of resources, especially their practical contributions to teaching.

A. Maps and globes

The globe is a more accurate representation of the earth than a map, and one might think that it would be introduced first in the elementary school. As a matter of fact, some of the teacher manuals on this topic deal with the globe first and then with maps. On the other hand, it is rather obvious that in order for a youngster in the lower grade levels to understand that the globe is a representation or a map of the earth, he should have first a notion of what a map is. He can develop this notion primarily by going through a systematic process of learning how to make a map of his local environment. It is difficult and rather impractical to separate the treatment of maps and globes; they complement each other. In this section maps and globes will be presented together in terms of reading and understanding them, and in terms of their variety and their uses in developing concepts and generalizations.

READING AND UNDERSTANDING MAPS AND GLOBES

In order for someone to be able to read and understand maps and globes he must develop a number of related abilities, skills and concepts in a sequential order. In a recent book, Hanna and others suggest that the following abilities and understandings be developed in children to enable them to read and understand maps:

1. The ability to observe systematically and to identify and note the location and distribution and density of features of the landscape.
2. The ability to orient self and to note directions in space and on maps.
3. The ability to locate places, distributions, and densities on maps.
4. The ability to use scale and to judge or measure distance in space and on maps.
5. The ability to use and understand symbols and to visualize the realities for which they stand.
6. The ability to use cartographic principles of map composition and graphic expression.
7. The ability to recognize and express relative location.
8. The ability to use and understand basic map projections.
9. The ability to understand and relate areal distributions.
10. The ability to use and understand the globe as a model of the earth.[1]

---

[1] Paul R. Hanna, Rose E. Sabaroff, Gordon F. Davies, and Charles R. Farrar, *Geography in the Teaching of Social Studies—Concepts and Skills* (Boston: Houghton Mifflin Co., 1966), p. 12.

Each item in the above list has been expanded by the authors in order to provide more specific direction to the teacher. Since space does not permit inclusion of the details here, teachers and school administrators are urged to examine the book carefully.

In connection with the last item in the above list, the same authors suggest the following understandings concerning the globe as a model of the earth:

1. The globe is a spherically shaped model of the earth.
2. The shape of the earth is round in every direction.
3. The globe shows the earth's natural features such as the land and water masses, and some globes show some of the cultural features.
4. A system of grid lines is drawn on the surface of the globe— north-south lines and east-west lines.
5. The grid system provides the means of locating places on the globe surface.
6. North and South are definite points on the globe (the North and the South Poles), whereas east and west are not definite points.
7. The cardinal directions are read along the grid lines of the globe.
8. A great circle divides the globe into two equal parts.
9. Global distances are measured along great circle-routes.
10. The shortest distance between two points is along the great circle.
11. The earth turns (rotates) on its axis.
12. The turning or rotation of the earth gives us day and night.
13. The earth's revolving around the sun gives us the seasons.
14. The map of the world on the curved surface of the globe is the only exact map we have.
15. The surface of any spheroidal subject cannot be flattened (made into a map) without breaking and stretching parts of it. This is called distortion.
16. The transfer or projection of any large area of a globe to a flat surface (a map) results in some distortion.[2]

Needless to say that in order for the youngsters to develop the abilities and concepts listed in both of the above lists, they should be

---

[2] *Ibid.*, p. 43.

involved in appropriate activities. It would take volumes to list and elaborate every one of these activities. As a compromise, some of the basic sources are listed here in which the activities or samples of activities can be found. Included in the sources are research studies related to map reading and understanding as well.

1. Anderzhon, Mamie L., "Globe-Centered Classroom," *The Grade Teacher*. Volume 79 (September 1962), pp. 140–143.

2. Anderzhon, Mamie L., "Three Billion People—Where Do They Live?" *The Grade Teacher*. Volume 80 (June 1963), pp. 46–47.

3. Anderzhon, Mamie L. *Steps in Map Reading*. (Chicago: Rand McNally and Co., 1955).

4. Davies, Gordon Francis, "Map Skills and Understandings in Intermediate School Social Studies," *Dissertation Abstracts*. Volume 23 (September 1962), pp. 948–949.

5. Davis, O. L., "Learning about Time Zones in Grades Four, Five, and Six," *The Journal of Experimental Education*. Volume 31 (May 1963), pp. 407–412.

6. Farrar, Charles Robert, "Map Skills and Understandings in Upper Elementary School Social Studies," *Dissertation Abstracts*. Volume 24 (September 1963), pp. 1094–1095.

7. Griffin, Paul F., and Freeman, Robert R., *Map and Globe Activities for Children*. (San Francisco: Fearon Publisher, Inc., 1953).

8. Hanna, Paul R., Sabaroff, Rose E., Davies, Gordon F., and Farrar, Charles R., "Geographic Content and Map Skills," (Chapter 1), *Geography in the Teaching of Social Studies—Concepts and Skills*. (Boston: Houghton Mifflin Company, 1966), pp. 5–46.

9. Harris, Rudy M., *Handbook of Map and Globe Usage*. (New York: Rand McNally and Co., 1959).

10. Jarolimek, John, "Teaching Children the Use of Globes and Maps," (Chapter 10), *Social Studies in Elementary Education*. Third edition. (New York: The Macmillan Company, 1967), pp. 270–300.

11. Joyce, William W., "The Development and Grade Placement of Map and Globe Skills in the Elementary Social Studies Program," *Dissertation Abstracts*. Volume 2 (May 1963), pp. 6434–6435.

12. Kohn, Clyde, "Interpreting Maps and Globes," *Skills in Social Studies*. Twenty-fourth Yearbook, National Council for the Social Studies (Washington: NCSS, 1953), pp. 166–167.

13. McAulay, John D., "Some Map Abilities of Second Grade Children," *The Journal of Geography*. Volume 6 (January 1962), pp. 3–9.

14. McAulay, John D., "Map Learnings in the Fourth Grade," *The Journal of Geography*, Volume 63 (March 1964), pp. 123–127.

15. Michaelis, John U., "Maps and Globes," Chapter 13. *Social Studies for Children in a Democracy*. Third edition. (Englewood Cliffs, N. J.: Prentice-Hall, Inc., 1963), pp. 403–444.

16. Rushdoony, Haiz A., "Achievement in Map-Reading: An Experimental Study," *The Elementary School Journal*. Volume 64 (November 1963), pp. 70–75.

17. Sabaroff, Rose, "Improving the Use of Maps in the Elementary School," *Journal of Geography*. Volume 60 (April 1961), pp. 184–190.

18. Whipple, Gertrude, "Geography in the Elementary Social Studies Program," *New Viewpoints in Geography*. Twenty-ninth Yearbook, National Council for the Social Studies (Washington, D. C.: NCSS, 1959), pp. 112–143.

VARIETY OF MAPS AND GLOBES

The first gross classification of maps and globes is on the basis of whether they are two-dimensional or three-dimensional. The two-dimensional or the flat maps and the globes with smooth surface are more abstract than the raised relief maps and globes. Relief maps and globes are good for showing the physical characteristics of an area and they are more difficult to make. Therefore, they are more expensive.

The two-dimensional maps and globes, especially the maps, are classified into slated, physical, political, and special purpose maps. The slated maps and globes simply outline the major land areas and borderlines and are very useful for class exercises. The physical maps and globes outline land and water areas by using different colors to show varied elevations of land and sea depths. There are conventional colors to be used, but cartographers appear to be moving away from conventional colors, towards the idea of using natural colors with a clear legend. It is better to teach the youngsters how to read and use the legend rather than memorize the various so-called conventional colors. The political maps and globes show the boundaries of various nations which are distinguished from each other through one-tone contrasting colors. Major cities, rivers, and transportation routs are usually shown on political maps or globes.

Special purpose maps most commonly found in schools include climate maps, economic maps, population maps, historical maps, world geography maps, literature maps, and others. Many of the special purpose maps come in sets such as the "Our American History Maps," the "World History" maps, and "World Geography" maps published by Denoyer-Geppert Company.

Another practical way to classify maps and globes is on the basis of their difficulty level. Some maps and globes are simple, without too much information, so that they can be used with young children to learn basic information such as land and water masses, major rivers, the shape and location of various countries and states, the location of major cities and similar information. The maps and globes used in the upper grades have too much information on them and they could be very confusing to the young child.

Included among the maps are some very useful charts. Among the most important are the "Geographical Terms" and "Our Democracy" charts. The geographical terms chart comes in two-dimensional as well as in three-dimensional form. Also, teachers should be aware of the availability of the variety of rather inexpensive desk outline maps. They are very useful for various exercises.

It is recommended that teachers become familiar with the great variety of maps and globes which, indeed, can make their teaching of social studies much easier and more meaningful. One way to achieve this familiarization is by examining the catalogues which the various companies publish. Some of the main companies are:

1. American Map Company, 11 West 46th Street, New York, New York.
2. Aero-Service Corporation, 236 East Courtland street, Philadelphia, Pennsylvania. (Good source for relief maps and globes).
3. George F. Cram Co., Inc., 730 East Washington Street, Indianapolis, Indiana.

4. Denoyer-Geppert Company, 5235 Ravenswood Avenue, Chicago, Illinois.
5. A. J. Nystrom and Company, 333 Elston Avenue, Chicago, Illinois.
6. Rand McNally and Company, P. O. Box 7800, Chicago, Illinois.
7. Replogle Globes, 315 Hoyne Avenue, Chicago, Illinois.
8. Universal Map Co., Inc., 22 Park Place, New York, New York.
9. Webster Costello Co., Chicago Heights, Illinois.

USING MAPS AND GLOBES

One particular primary grade teacher devoted a considerable amount of time helping the children to develop some understanding of the generalization, "Life on earth is influenced by the earth's (global) shape, its size and its set of motions." She planned a good number of lessons in order to achieve this and she used a variety of instructional materials. One of the specific objectives related to the generalization was the understanding that the rotation of the earth around its axis causes day and night. In other to reach this specific objective the teacher utilized a globe and a flashlight. In a semidark room she shined the flashlight representing the sun, on the globe. The children could clearly see that half of the globe was bright and half dark. They were asked to determine if the United States was on the dark side. Also, the children were asked to make a list of possible night activities as well as a list of possible day activities.

Another teacher was attempting through the study of Japan to illustrate the generalization, "Geographical features influence man's way of living." The teacher showed a relief map of Japan so that the children could witness the fact that the mountainous terrain did not lend itself to large-scale agriculture. After a short discussion the children concluded that this was one of the major reasons why the Japanese turned to industry.

A third teacher was in the process of developing the generalization, "Man constantly seeks to satisfy his needs for food, clothing and shelter, and his other wants; in so doing, he attempts to adapt, shape, utilize, and exploit the earth." In order to demonstrate the relationship inherent in this generalization the teacher used a series of maps to show the development of the local community in the last one hundred years. She pointed out that the town was very small at first and occupied only the present downtown area. In some of the present outlining neighborhoods there was a huge forest which was cut down to make room for housing as well as to provide lumber. The children learned that small hills were leveled to make room for shopping plazas as well as to facilitate transportation.

There is an unlimited number of ways in which globes and maps can be used to help teach social studies, especially when the concept approach is used. This section will be concluded with one more illustration. A first-grade teacher was building a number of lessons around the generalization, "Interdependence has been a constant factor in human relationships everywhere." In connection with these lessons she placed a world map in front of the children and pointed out the places around the world where we obtain natural resources and how important it is that we have a mutual friendship with these peoples.

B. Other audio-visual aids

Never before in history and probably nowhere else in the world today do teachers of social studies have at their disposal the variety and quality of audio-visual aids which the American teacher now has. "There is scarcely a unit in the social studies that cannot be vitalized through a useful free film," wrote William H. Hartley a few years ago.[3] The same applies for filmstrips, audio-tapes and a host of other materials.

Psychologists tell us, and common knowledge verifies, that the more senses the child uses in acquiring learnings, the more he learns and the more permanent his learnings are. The question is no longer whether audiovisual aids are useful or not; this has been answered in the affirmative conclusively. The problem is how the teacher can keep up with all that is being produced and how she can use it effectively so that her class will move faster towards the achievement of its educational goals.

The remainder of this chapter is devoted to assisting teachers with this problem. First, the variety of audio-visual aids will be pre-

---

[3] William H. Hartley, "Vitalizing the Social Studies," in: John R. Lee and Jonathon C. McLendon, *Readings on Elementary Social Studies* (Boston: Allyn and Bacon, Inc., 1965), p. 378.

sented. Then, a list of sources of audio-visual materials will be given. Following that, some suggestions will be offered concerning the proper use of these materials. Finally, some illustrations of the uses of audio-visual materials will be given.

VARIETY OF AUDIO-VISUAL AIDS

A list of audio-visual aids includes the following materials and equipment:

Films	Records
Filmstrips	Tape-recordings
Slides	Bulletin boards and flannel boards
Pictures	Radio
Photographs	Television
Illustrations	Moving projector
Transparancies	Filmstrip and slide projector
Video-tapes	Overhead projector
Realia of all kinds	Opaque projector
Models	Various duplicating machines

There are very few schools today which do not have a good stock of the materials listed above and most of the equipment. Those schools lagging behind should appoint a committee to look into the matter and suggest the purchase of these materials and equipment as priority items in the next budget. It should also be pointed out that some of these materials can be prepared locally by the teacher and class.

SOURCES OF AUDIO-VISUAL AIDS

The sources of audio-visual aids are too many to list exhaustively. The list presented here is partial and represents mainly those sources used by the faculty of one particular school. It should be pointed out that this listing includes for the most part comprehensive sources and only a few companies with limited productions. In most cases the titles of the sources indicate the types of materials.

1. *Blue Book of Audio-Visual Materials.* 64 E. Lake St., Chicago: Educational Screen.
2. *Complete Index of Educational Filmstrips.* 2338 E. Johnson St., Madison, Wisc.: Filmstrip Distributors.
3. Compton's Picture Library. 1000 N. Dearborn St., Chicago, Ill. 60610.

4. Coronet Films. Coronet Building, Chicago, Ill. 60601.
5. *Educational Film Guide.* 950 University Ave., New York, N. Y. 10052.
6. *Educational Guide to Free Tapes, Scripts, and Transcriptions.* Randolph, Wisc.: Educators Progress Service.
7. Encyclopedia Britannica Films, Inc. 1150 Wilmette Ave., Wilmette, Ill.
8. *Filmstrip Guide.* 950 University Ave., New York, N. Y. 10052.
9. Folkways Record and Service Corporation. 117 W. 46th St., New York, N. Y. 10036.
10. *Guides to Newer Educational Media: Films, Filmstrips, Phonorecords, Radio, Slides, T. V.* 50 E. Huron St., Chicago, Ill. 60611: American Library Association.
11. Informative Classroom Publishers. 40 Ionis Ave., N. W. Grand Rapids, Mich.
12. *Life* Filmstrips. Time—Life Building, Rockefeller Center, New York, N. Y. 10020.
13. *Listings of Educational Recordings and Filmstrips for more Effective Learning.* 1730 "I" St., N. W., Washington, D. C.: Educational Services.
14. *Materials for the New Social Studies, 1967.* 4455 Lennox Boulevard, Inglewood, Cal. 90304: Social Studies School Service.
15. *Modern Index and Guide to Free Educational Films from Industry.* 45 Rockefeller Plaza, New York, N. Y. 10020: Modern Teaching Picture Service.
16. *Recordings for Education: Social Studies.* 797 Seventh Ave., New York, N. Y. 10019: Columbia Records.
17. *Social Studies: Films and Filmstrips.* 332 S. Michigan Avenue, Chicago, Ill. 60604: International Film Bureau, Inc.
18. Stanley Bowmar Co., Inc. 15 Cleveland St., Valhalla, N. Y.
19. *The American Film Review.* Eastern Baptist College, St. Davids, Pa.: The American Educational and Historical Film Center.
20. *The Educators Guide to Free Films.* Randolph, Wisc.: Educators Progress Service.
21. *The Educational Media Index.* 330 W. 42nd St., New York, N.Y. 10036: McGraw-Hill Book Company, Inc.
22. *U. S. Government Films for Public Educational Use.* Washington, D. C.: U. S. Government Printing Office.
23. Visual Products Division, 3M Company. 2501 Hudson Road, St. Paul, Minn. 55119 (Mostly transparancies and printed spirit masters).

24. Visual Specialties Company. 5701 W. Vernon St., Detroit, Mich. (mostly materials for flannel boards).

A school or even a teacher could secure a good supply of catalogues, free of charge, by writing to individual companies. Though only the major companies are listed above, the others can be located in the comprehensive listings.

A good source for more recent audio-visual aids is also *Social Education*, the journal of the National Council for the Social Studies. Every month they publish a section entitled "Sight and Sound." The most recent films, filmstrips and social studies materials are described and reviewed.

One thing is clear, no teacher can say that she is not using audio-visual aids because there are not enough of them or because she cannot locate them.

Effective Use of Audio-Visual Aids

Audio-visual aids are used to do what words alone cannot do. They are capable of breaking the bariers of time and space to bring into the sphere of the child's experience that which would otherwise remain distant and remote. Audio-visual aids make possible differentiation of instruction and, therefore, accommodate individual differences.

Audio-visual aids usually serve three basic instructional purposes:

1. They are used to motivate the students to the study of a new area, new concept or new generalization.
2. They are used as sources of specific knowledge or as means for demonstrating relationships in the formation of concepts and generalizations.
3. They are used to summarize a unit or to assist pupils in evaluating what they have learned from other sources.

For audio-visual aids to fulfill their role, their selection must be made carefully, based on determined educational objectives, and used within a preplanned pattern. There are teachers who use audio-visual aids because they want to show the principal that they are skilled with modern methodological procedures. They order a few films each semester and show them whenever the principal comes. Others keep on stock a number of filmstrips and show them to fill a poorly planned period or to keep the children quiet during noon recess.

For some teachers, maps, globes, charts and other manipulative materials serve as decorative objects on the walls and shelves around the room.

Ineffective use of audio-visual aids is also witnessed on a large scale. Recently the author participated in a conference to assess the value of teaching social studies through educational television. Twelve social studies specialists from across the country viewed and evaluated over seventy telecourses submitted by the majority of the nation's nearly 120 educational television stations.

The general impression which the specialists formed was rather negative. Considerable amounts of money were spent to produce television programs which were intended not to assist the teacher by bringing to the class that which she cannot bring, but to provide instead a poor substitute for her. Most programs were descriptive in nature and did not include the most recent trends in social studies education. The specialists agreed that the teaching of social studies through television must, under proper leadership, assume a new direction.

Effective use of audio-visual aids demands a well planned program, an awareness of available materials and equipment, and a number of specific skills. The National Council for the Social Studies, to make teachers aware of the skills needed and to assist them in developing these skills, published a number of related pamphlets in the "How to Do It Series." Among these are:

1. *How to Use a Motion Picture.*
2. *How to Use a Bulletin Board.*
3. *How to Use Recordings.*

Other sources, such as the following, may serve the same purpose:

1. *E-Z Bulletin Boards* by Anne D. Weseloh. San Francisco, California: Fearon, Publishers, 1959.
2. *Felt-Boards for Teaching* by Charles Dent and Ernest Tiemann. Austin, Texas: Division of Extension, University of Texas, 1957.
3. "Flannel Boards in Action" by Milton E. Crassell. *Educational Screen and Audio-Visual Guide.* Volume 34 (June 1955), pp. 250–251.
4. *Handbook for Graphic Presentation* by Calvin F. Schmid. New York: Ronald Press Co., 1954.
5. *Learning from Pictures* by Catharine Williams. Washington,

D. C.: Department of Audio-visual Instruction, National
Education Association, 1963.

All sources listed above agree that the teacher using audio-visual
aids must follow certain general rules which fall into three catagories:
what the teacher must do before using the aid, during the use of the
aid, and as follow-up activities.

In preparing herself the teacher must become very familiar with
the aid. If it is a film or a filmstrip, for example, she must preview it
and take notes. Furthermore, the teacher should make sure that the
aid fits her objectives as well as the ability and interest levels of the children. Also, she should prepare questions which will help the children
understand the concepts the film reinforces as they watch it. Needless
to say, the mechanical aspects of preparation are also important.

During use of the aid, the teacher should control all factors in the
environment which might distract the youngsters such as light, ventila-
tion and the like. In the case of a demonstration, the teacher should
make sure that all children can observe. While it is advisable for her
to take advantage of the so-called teachable moments, she should
direct the activity towards those concepts and understandings for which
the aid was selected.

Finally, there should be follow-up activities in which the children
will clearly see the relationship between the aid and the objective.
They may include discussions, answering a number of questions, and
comparing one particular aid with another.

Illustrations on the Utilization of Audio-Visual Aids

A second-grade teacher based a number of her lessons on the
generalization, "Interdependence has been a constant and important
factor in human relationships everywhere." In order to stress the concept of interdependence she showed the film *Where Does Our Food Come
From?* produced by Coronet Instructional Films.

A fourth-grade teacher was attempting to prove to the children
that, "Although certain historical customs and institutions have characterized individual civilizations or nations in the past, men in every
age and place have made use of basic social functions in adjusting
themselves to their world." One of the aids which she used in this
effort was a series of filmstrips entitled *Boys and Girls of Many Lands*

produced by the Society for Visual Education. Through this series the teacher tried to draw the attention of the children to the fact that all cultures consider the education of the young to be a very important function.

A third-grade teacher tried to develop the basic generalization, "The world is shrinking in distance and time." She thought that the best way to show the important meaning of this generalization would be to expose the children to the modern means of communication media and make them aware of their effect in making the world smaller. As her first activity, she directed the children to various popular magazines and advertisement catalogues to find and cut out pictures of various modern means of communication. All these clippings were, then, arranged on the bulletin board with their names and dates of invention. The bulletin board served as a reference and starting point for many discussions and other activities.

A kindergarten teacher was giving her youngsters information which could be used later to develop the generalization, "Life on earth is influenced by the earth's (global) shape, its size, and its set of motions." She divided the bulletin board in four sections and labeled each one of them SPRING, SUMMER, FALL, WINTER. Then she showed to the children a collection of pictures, each depicting a scene from the lives of people during the various seasons. The children were asked to place each picture on the appropriate section of the bulletin board. The discussion during this lesson was lively and the whole lesson was fascinating.

Finally, a first-grade teacher used a model of a farm to explain to the students the role which each member of the family plays in order to maintain and operate the farm. This activity was undertaken in connection with the generalization, "The work of society is performed through organized groups. Group membership requires that individuals undertake varied roles involving differing responsibilities, rights and opportunities."

Charts, Graphs, and Tables

A section on audio-visual materials cannot be complete without some special reference to graphic materials. With the emphasis now placed on the skills of analyzing, interpreting, integrating, and forming generalizations, graphic materials such as charts, graphs, and tables have become very important. Charts are a key element in Hilda Taba's strategies for teaching and learning social studies.[4]

In studying about South America, for instance, Taba suggests that the class be organized in committees and the responsibility for each committee should be to collect information on a particular country in terms of the following topics: people, education, language, area, family structure, centers of population, work of people, chief exports and buyers, and imports and importers. All these data are then put on a single chart as follows:

	Brazil	*Argentina*	*etc.*
People	European—62% Mestizo—26% Negro—11% Others—1% Pop. 78,000,000	European—97% Indian and others—3% Pop. 22,000,000	
Education	Literacy—62% etc.	Literacy—92% etc.	
etc.			

Taba calls a chart like this a data retrieval chart and with the help of appropriate questions the children contrast and compare the information about the various countries in order to draw implications and make inferences.

Charts, graphs, and tables provide three of the most useful ways of organizing information for purposes of comparison, but they are highly abstract devices. In the past, graphic materials were not even considered to be appropriate for use with children in the lower grades. This view has changed recently, and the teaching of graphic materials should begin early in the elementary school and should be done meaningfully through actual experiences.

Charts, for example, may be introduced in the primary grades by making a list of the types of food we eat and then determining through discussion those produced locally and those from some other place. A chart like this is usually labeled as a classification chart. Other types of charts are made for the purpose of tabulating items, recording group

---

[4] Hilda Taba, *Teachers' Handbook for Elementary Social Studies* (Palo Alto: Addison-Wesley Publishing Company, 1967), pp. 63–72.

standards and experiences, showing the flow of sequences and events diagrammatically and for other reasons.

Graphs can be used for a variety of experiences. Bar graphs can be produced to show, for instance, the enrollment in each grade or in a particular school in the last ten years. Circle graphs, pictorial graphs, and line graphs are used to show relationships.

Tables provide another convenient way to organize information. In a rather detailed chapter on graphic materials, Michaelis wrote: "Tables are a concise way of presenting related quantitative information. Facts or figures are arranged in columns or rows for fast reading and for making comparisons."[5] For example, the various steel producing countries may be listed in one column and the amount of steel they produce in another. The industrial status of these countries can be formulated based on such tables.

SUMMARY

Any conscientious teacher would consider it impossible today to teach social studies without the use of maps and other audio-visual aids such as films, filmstrips, pictures, models, radio, television and the like. The value of all these aids, when used properly, has been demonstrated beyond doubt. This chapter was intended to assist the teacher in utilizing aids effectively by offering suggestions and providing related information.

First, it is strongly recommended that teachers should familiarize themselves with the wide variety of existing maps, globes and other aids. Various sources were suggested to assist in this task.

Second, the use of audio-visual aids requires the development of specific skills on the part of the teacher as well as on the part of the children. In order for children to use maps and globes, for instance, they should develop certain skills and concepts. Specific sources of practical information on the development of these skills and concepts are listed.

Finally, the teacher should use the various aids only when needed to fulfill educational objectives. A number of illustrations are provided to demonstrate how teachers utilized various aids with their classes in order to achieve specific educational objectives.

---

[5] John U. Michaelis, *Social Studies for Children in a Democracy*, Third edition (Englewood Cliffs, N.J.: Prentice-Hall, Inc., 1963), p. 390.

Capitalizing on Current Events and Dramatic Exercises

8

Capitalizing on Current Events
and Dramatic Exercises

Current events and dramatic activities can enrich social studies instruction and substantially aid the transmission of knowledge and the development of commitments and skills. Social studies at the elementary level teaches the youngsters about society and how to lead a successful life in it. This statement implies that current events, events occurring within contemporary society, cannot be ignored and their significance should not be minimized.

It further implies the development of certain interests, attitudes, and dispositions. This demands self-expression on the part of the children and the involvement of their inner world in classroom experiences. Well directed activities involving dramatics, music, and rhythm are most helpful in achieving these aims.

A. Current events

Current events, contemporary events, current affairs, or contemporary affairs are terms used as synonyms. At one of the recent meetings of the National Council for the Social Studies, current events were termed emerging social realities effecting institutions. This definition implies that current events take place at the local level as well as at the state, national, and world levels.

The terms *world affairs* and *world events* are also occasionally used to mean current events. These terms are not the best substitutes because *world events* or *world affairs* imply events or affairs with a world-wide effect.

VALUES IN UTILIZING CURRENT EVENTS

It was advocated elsewhere in this book that social studies in the elementary school should be geared towards the understanding of human relationships during the present time. The past is utilized as it is needed in the development of this understanding. This is a functional and dynamic approach to social studies, and a conscious effort to keep current events in the fore will undoubtedly assist in making this approach effective. This first value of current events, therefore, stems from the fact that the study of current events contributes towards making contemporary society the center of social studies.

Dealing with the contemporary scene makes it possible to bridge the gap between the formal classroom environment and the outside world in which the child spends a considerable amount of his time and with which many of his interests are associated. The child comes to school to develop concepts, generalizations, skills and commitments. The development of all these becomes easier when the child's centers of interest are involved. Current events often constitute important centers of children's interests. They make another significant contribution when they cause school learnings, which are in the most part abstract, to become more concrete.

Furthermore, the constant utilization of current events promotes the child's interest in what is going on around him and makes him more conscious of social realities and their basic characteristic, changeability. In our times we cannot afford a citizenry which is ignorant, indifferent, or apathetic to the ills and hopes of our society and the world.

CURRENT EVENTS AND THE SOCIAL STUDIES PROGRAM

There is a variety of ways in which current events have been or are being used in the classroom. Some of these ways appear to be sound within the total context of the social studies program while others go contrary to the scope of a sound program and the method of presenting it. An attempt will be made to describe the various ways of presenting current events and a recommendation will be given of the one most in harmony with the social studies program as conceived within the pages of this book.

Current events as a separate entity. In some schools current events are taught in addition to the social studies program. A period is set aside during which the youngsters discuss or report on current events, or read from a special current events magazine or the local paper. Once a week children are usually tested on what happened during that week.

The validity of this method can be challenged on several grounds. In the first place, the curriculum of the elementary school is crowded. If new elements could be incorporated within the present program without adding new periods, they would be more easily accommodated. Current events are so much a part of social studies that it seems illogical to teach them separately. Furthermore, an observation of separate current events classes reveals evidence which discourages the practice. In most cases the study of current events becomes a routine, dry affair which the children dislike. For many children the current events lesson consists of reading the current events weekly magazine and taking a test on it. Furthermore, current events may be unrelated to each other and when they are taught separately it is in many cases difficult for the teacher to unify them and make them meaningful for the children.

Current events as the basis for social studies. Other schools have tried to combine social studies and current events by basing the structure of social studies on current happenings. Some of the basic issues and significant events of the times became major unit topics. This might have been the right approach more than ten years ago, but not now. At the present time the emphasis is towards a more solid organization of the content of social studies which cannot be based on something as unpredictable and flexible as current events and issues. The organization desired today should be based on the fundamentals of the organized disciplines of the social sciences. Accepting current events as the basis for the social studies program is to go contrary to the type of social studies program advocated throughout this book.

Current events as a resource. The best way to use current events is to look upon them as a vital resource, as a means through which the development of predetermined concepts and generalizations can be assisted. For instance, one particular teacher would like to teach the concept of change in society. In order for the children to develop this concept the teacher must expose them to as many specific instances of social change as possible. Since social change is usually manifested in the form of changes in social institutions, the teacher might direct the children to books and films and other resources to learn about such changes in the past. But she can also direct them to current changes in social institutions such as the overthrow of a democratic regime and the establishment of a dictatorship or the establishment of an independent nation.

The recommendation that current events become a resource in the teaching of a preplanned substantive program should not give rise to the belief that they are not important or that they should be dealt with in a casual way. It is hoped that teachers will make every effort to relate all important current issues and events to the regular program. If an important issue emerges or a significant event takes place and it cannot be tied to the regular program, the teacher should deal with it independently and later try to relate it to the regular program. This, obviously, is completely different from the practice of allocating a period a day during which the class searches for current events to fulfill the demands of a routine.

Also, the lack of a regularly scheduled current events period should not mean that the teacher refrain from a constant effort to indirectly alert the youngsters to current events. The classroom environment should be properly arranged, through the use of news maps and other materials, so that it can stimulate the children towards current happenings. A variety of news magazines and newspapers should be available for the children to browse through whenever they have an opportunity. Products of current events activities, undertaken in class in relation to the regular social studies program, should be displayed. The teacher's example can be the best inspiration for children. Parents should be encouraged to discuss current events and allow the children to participate. Also, parents should be encouraged to have news magazines and newspapers around the house and, at least once a day, watch and listen to a major news broadcast.

CURRENT EVENTS ACTIVITIES

In the process of utilizing current events to develop concepts and generalizations the teacher may engage the children in a variety of activities. John Jarolimek suggests the following list:

1. Round table discussions
2. Panel discussions
3. Making charts, maps, graphs
4. Constructing posters, murals
5. Keeping scrapbooks of news stories or pictures
6. Drawing cartoons to illustrate news
7. Giving reports
8. Conducting radio news programs
9. Dramatizing news events
10. Listening to live radio broadcasts
11. Viewing telecasts of special events.[1]

CURRENT EVENTS RESOURCES

Included below are resources to be used by the teacher as well as sources of materials designed for the children. An effort was made to include sources of materials designed exclusively for the elementary school. Some resources for secondary school materials have also been included with the hope that they can be of assistance to the elementary teacher as well.

RESOURCES FOR THE TEACHER:

1. Books and Pamphlets:

   a. All social studies education books include a chapter or a section on current events.

   b. Pearson, Craig and Patrick Whalen, ed., *Current Affairs in Today's Social Studies*. (Middletown, Connecticut: American Education Publications, Inc., 1965).

2. Periodical Articles:

   a. Connor, William H. "When Teaching Current Affairs: Nine Suggestions," *Social Education*. Volume 19 (November 1955), pp. 306–308.

   b. Criscuolo, Anthony, "Current Events in the Classroom," *The Elementary School Journal*. Volume 63 (May 1963), pp. 427–429.

---

[1] John Jarolimek, *Social Studies in Elementary Education*. Third edition (New York: The Macmillan Company, 1967), pp. 392–393.

c. Doering, Anita L., "How Can We Make the Teaching of Current Affairs Interesting and Effective?", *The Social Studies*. Volume 42 (December 1951), pp. 336–338.

d. Entin, Jack W., "Using Cartoons in the Classroom," *Social Education*. Volume 22 (May 1958), p. 241.

e. McAulay, John D., "Current Affairs and the Social Studies," *Social Education*. Volume 23 (January 1959), pp. 21–22.

f. McLendon, Jonathan C., "Using Daily Newspapers More Effectively," *Social Education*. Volume 23 (October 1959), pp. 263–265.

g. Schminke, Clarence William, "A Study of the Effective Utilization of a Classroom Newsmagazine in Teaching Current Events," *Dissertation Abstracts*. Volume 21 (January–March 1961), pp. 1874–1875.

h. Smith, Lloyd L., "Current Events for Elementary Schools," *Social Education*. Volume 25 (February 1961), pp. 75–78, 81.

i. Wass, Philmore B., "Improving Current Events Instruction," *Social Education*. Volume 25 (February 1961), pp. 79–81.

j. Wilson, Richard, "Using News to Teach Geography," *Social Education*. Volume 24 (February 1960), pp. 56–57.

RESOURCES FOR USE WITH THE CHILDREN:

1. *Periodicals:*

a. *My Weekly Reader*, Grades 1–6. American Education Press, Educational Center, Columbus, Ohio 43216.

b. *News Pilot*, Grade 1; *News Ranger*, Grade 2; *News Trail*, Grade 3; *News Explorer*, Grade 4; *Newstime*, Grades 5 and 6. Scholastic Magazines, 33 W. 42nd Street, New York 10036.

2. *Newsmaps:*

a. "World News of the Week," by News Map of the Week, 7300 N. Linden Avenue, Skokie, Illinois 60076.

b. *Time* and *Newsweek* magazines also provide subscribing classes with special current events maps and charts.

3. *Filmstrips:*

a. Current Affairs Films, 527 Madison Avenue, New York, New York 10022. This company produces a filmstrip a month on current issues and events and distributes it to fifty sponsored areas through local newspapers and banks. For the name of the sponsoring newspaper or bank in your area write directly to the company.

b. The New York Times Company, Office of Educational Activities, Times Square, New York, New York 10036. The New York Times issues monthly during the school year a filmstrip which deals with important topics in the news. Each strip treats a single topic that is in the public eye. A discussion manual is provided along with each filmstrip.

c. "VEC News Program" by Visual Education Consultants, Inc., P. O. Box 52, Madison, Wisconsin 53701. VEC issues one filmstrip a week. A filmstrip entitled "What's Going On?" is sent to the teacher free of charge for orientation purposes.

CONTROVERSIAL ISSUES IN THE ELEMENTARY SCHOOL

A section on current events will not be complete without any reference to controversial issues and their place in the elementary school classroom. If social studies is to present a realistic picture of our contemporary society it is impossible to leave controversial issues outside the classroom. Controversial issues are an essential part of social studies. Teachers at all levels must deal with them.

It is true that at times the teaching of controversial issues puts the teacher in a difficult position. This, however, should not be an excuse to avoid teaching issues which are of vital importance in the society in which the children are learning to live. It is time teachers and their organizations became professionally strong enough to neutralize the forces of bias and narrow interest.

Leonard Kenworthy[2] gives the following suggestions to the teacher dealing with controversial issues:

1. Establish in cooperation with the children some "ground rules" in regard to the classroom atmosphere and class conduct which should be maintained during the treatment of controversial issues.

2. Be sure that all sides of the question are presented.

3. Try to get students to separate facts from opinion.

---

[2] Leonard S. Kenworthy, *Guide to Social Studies Teaching.* Second edition (Belmont, California: Wadsworth Publishing Company, Inc., 1966), pp. 253–254.

4. Try to get students to understand points of view with which they disagree.
5. Don't encourage opinions not based on an adequate background.
6. Keep in mind the importance of suspended judgments. Conclusions do not have to be reached on all issues.
7. Help to develop critical thinking about controversial issues.
8. You may want to use a continuum to show the several points of view possible on a given issue.
9. It is sometimes important to have an introductory session in which the students can air their strong opinions freely.
10. Try to get students to read as much as possible.
11. If the discussion of a controversial issue gets out of hand, postpone it for another day.

Many times the question is asked: Should the teacher take a position on controversial issues? The teacher should guide the discussion according to the rules of reflective thinking and the suggestions listed above. If the class demands it, the teacher should express her opinion, provided she has one, and as long as it is made clear that it is an opinion. It is advisable, however, that the teacher give evidence to substantiate her position.

Classroom Illustrations of Current Events Utilization

A third-grade class was involved in activities which, it was hoped, would lead them to understand that "soils are altered by nature and man." In one of these activities the teacher utilized a recently completed irrigation system in the vicinity. She took the children to it and they were amazed at the difference in vegetation caused by irrigation. After a good discussion about the differences due to irrigation, the teacher asked why these changes had taken place. Through reflection the class was able to conclude that by bringing water, man was able to change the capacity of the soil to produce vegetation.

A sixth-grade teacher wanted to begin a series of specific studies for the purpose of leading the children to understand the generalization that "The evolution of mankind from isolated, self-sufficient communities to an interdependent whole means even more trade, migration, diffusion of ideas and practices, and greater importance of relative location or situation." As an initiation activity to these studies, this particular teacher discussed with the class the recent Immigration Law passed by Congress.

A fifth-grade teacher was attempting to lead her class to the understanding that "Democracy is based on such beliefs as the integrity of man, the dignity of the individual, equality of opportunity, man's rationality, man's morality, man's ability to govern himself and to solve his problems cooperatively." In this effort she engaged the class in the discussion of recent outbreaks of violence in American cities and tried to identify the causes of such lawlessness among the American people.

A kindergarten teacher was leading her youngsters towards the understanding that "Change has been a universal condition of human society." She knew that this understanding would not develop until much later, but she involved the youngsters in activities which showed groups of people leading a common way of life because they had things in common. Also she tried to show to the youngsters that when people live together things happen which modify their way of life. During one particular day, this teacher found out that a new baby was added in Dick's family. Dick was excited about it, as were his friends. She took the opportunity to engage the class in a discussion on how the new-born baby caused some changes in the way Dick's family was living before the baby was born.

B. Dramatic and rhythmic exercises

Dramatic and rhythmic exercises are, by themselves, simply fun. However, this is not the primary reason why they are considered important in the teaching of social studies. Their value for the social studies teacher stems from the fact that because they are fun they contribute in the achievement of social studies objectives. As Bost and Martin[3] demonstrated through a related study, dramatic exercises assist children in clarifying what they call physical, social, and moral realities. The first thing to remember, then, is that dramatics and rhythm, like all other resources, are not ends in themselves but means through which to achieve other specific ends. Beginning with this assumption makes a difference as to how far and in what direction a teacher can go with dramatic and rhythmic exercises.

---

[3] Theda K. Bost and Clyde Martin, "The Role of Dramatic Play in the Young Child's Clarification of Reality," *The Elementary School Journal*. Volume 57 (February 1957), pp. 276–280.

Types of Dramatic and Rhythmic Exercises

In the early grades dramatic exercises take the form of *informal dramatic play*. Children at this level are more uninhibited than at later stages of development and enjoy playing the role of characters whom they study. Dramatic play is spontaneous. It gives an opportunity to the child to identify with a particular character and portray him as he understands the person's role and behavior.

As children grow and pass into the intermediate grades, they become more inhibited and dramatic play does not appeal to them as much. At this stage they are ready for a more *formal dramatization* with script, costumes, stage and audience. In many cases the children write their own plays on the basis of what they have studied.

Another form of dramatic exercise with more affective than cognitive implications is *role-playing* or *sociodrama*. Shaftel and Shaftel characterize role-playing as a basic social studies process because they perceive it as a process through which the children exercise inquiry and modify their values. In their words:

> Through role-playing of typical conflict situations, children and young people can be helped to articulate the ways in which they tend to solve their problems. In the enactments, the consequences (social and personal) of the choices they make become more explicit. Analyses of these choices can lay bare the values underlying each line of action. Young people can thus learn that they act (make decisions) on the basis of the values they hold, which may be consciously, but most often unconsciously, held. Once aware of their own valuing, they are in a position to modify their values.[4]

Puppetry is another form which dramatic exercises can take. It is less expensive in terms of costumes and stage settings and allows even the shy child to participate. A variety of inexpensive materials can be used to make dolls. These include tongue depressors stapled together, paper, paper bags, cloth and anything the ingenuity of the teacher dictates.

Included in the rhythmic exercises category are simple rhythmical movements accompanied by music and folk dances from all over the world. Both of these activities appeal to elementary school children.

---

[4] Fannie R. Shaftel and George Shaftel, *Role-Playing for Social Values: Decision-Making in the Social Studies* (Englewood Cliffs, N. J.: Prentice-Hall, Inc. 1967), p. 12.

The simple rhythmical activities appeal more to the younger child. Folk dancing is more complicated and demands more coordination. Older children can be more effective with it.

Also *pantomime* can be used as a form of dramatic exercise or even as a form of rhythmic exercise if it is accompanied by music. Children are good mimics and enjoy this activity. Pantomime provides a good basis for reflection and discussion of situations. It is a guessing game or a hypothesizing game in which the whole class participates.

Specific Functions of Dramatic and Rhythmic Exercises

One specific function of dramatic and rhythmic exercises could be to initiate the study of a particular topic or area. Think of a situation in which the teacher wants to initiate the development of some basic understanding in regard to Africa. She organizes the children to teach them an African folk dance. With drums beating and the children jumping, the class is already in Africa.

Involvement of dramatics and rhythm increases the interest of children in social studies. In a study completed by Cristiani,[5] social studies was rated initially as the first, second, or third choice by 34.27 percent of the children. At the close of the experiment and with the assistance of dramatization, the percentage of children who rated social studies as their first, second, or third choice rose to 50.70 percent.

Dramatic and rhythmic exercises also contribute in the development of deeper understandings. To prepare a skit on a historical or current social situation, for instance, requires considerable reading and close identification with the characters involved. All this means a better understanding of the situation at hand. Furthermore, dramatization helps the children develop democratic behavior and many of the social skills. It takes cooperation, discussion, intelligent decision making, and much self-discipline to dramatize a situation. Role-playing is especially useful as an instrument in developing attitudes and values important to democratic behavior.

In view of the individual differences in the classroom, dramatic and rhythmic exercises, like all other resources, are valuable in providing for variation of instructional procedure. It might be that the whole

---

[5] Vincent Anthony Cristiani, "Informal Dramatics in Social Studies," *Dissertation Abstracts*. Volume 21 (May 1961), p. 3375.

class is not interested in involving themselves in dramatics. It is available, though, for those who wish to do so.

On the other hand, there are situations in which dramatization may serve to help a class summarize or synthesize what they have learned. In unit teaching terminology, dramatics serves as a *culminating activity*. Culminating activities provide a good opportunity for the teacher to evaluate the children. Assisting the teacher in evaluation, therefore, should not be overlooked as a specific function of dramatic and rhythmic exercises.

Finally, dramatics and rhythm are valuable to the elementary teacher because they afford him with excellent opportunities for correlating social studies, English, and music. Since elementary teachers are responsible for the teaching of all subjects and in most cases they are pressed for time, this function is of great significance.

GUIDELINES FOR EFFECTIVE USE OF DRAMATIC AND RHYTHMIC EXERCISES

In the beginning of this section it was pointed out that dramatics and rhythm should not be used for their own sake. The understandings to be developed should be the basis for deciding the worth of a dramatic activity. If it takes too long or if the same understandings can be developed easier and better through some other method, dramatization should be avoided.

Stressing authenticity is one way to make dramatization more productive. This calls for careful reading by the children as well as analysis of what is read. If a scene during America's westward expansion is dramatized, in which a married couple is trying to decide whether to move west, the arguments between husband and wife should be true to that period. Children should not be allowed to say just anything. If costumes or scenery is to be prepared, the children should look for information which will help them be authentic. The children will search the literature with thirst and many concomitant learnings will result. It should be made a rule that every dramatic or rhythmic exercise must be based on a background of adequate knowledge. Even at the lower levels, at which the children cannot read well, dramatic play should follow a thorough discussion of the background.

The teacher should make an effort to assign roles to all children. The distribution of roles should be done according to interest and ability, but also according to need in terms of the attitudes or values which must be changed or developed in some children. If a child is aggressive, he should be put in a role in which he can experience the ugly effects of aggression. This might cause him to become less aggressive in everyday life.

TEACHER'S REFERENCES

Some of the most important references and sources for the teacher in dramatic and rhythmic exercises include the following:

1. Batchelder, Marjorie, *The Puppet Theatre Handbook* (New York: Harper and Brothers, 1947).
2. Bost, Theda Kirby and Clyde Martin, "The Role of Dramatic Play in the Young Child's Clarification of Reality," *The Elementary School Journal*. Volume 37 (February 1957), pp. 276–80.
3. Cristiani, Vincent Anthony, "Informal Dramatics in Social Studies," *Dissertation Abstracts*. Volume 21 (May 1961), p. 3375.
4. Dallmann, Martha, "The Role of Dramatics in the Social Studies," *Grade Teacher*. Volume 78 (April 1961), pp. 64–65.
5. Dugan, Ann S., *The Folk Dance Library* (New York: A. S. Barnes and Company, 1948), Five volumes.
6. Evans, Bessie, *American Indian Dance Steps* (New York: A. S. Barnes and Company, 1939).
7. Ryan, Grace L., *Dances of Our Pioneers* (New York: A. S. Barnes and Company, 1939).
8. Sehon, Elizabeth and Emma R. O'Brian, *Rhythm in Elementary Education* (New York: A. S. Barnes and Company, 1951).
9. Shaftel, Fannie R. and George Shaftel, *Role-Playing for Social Values: Decision-Making in the Social Studies* (Englewood Cliffs, N. J.: Prentice-Hall, Inc., 1967).
10. Siks, Geraldine Brain, "Third Grade Writes a Play," *Grade Teacher*. Volume 78 (September 1960), pp. 66–67.

ILLUSTRATIONS OF UTILIZATION OF DRAMATIC AND
RHYTHMIC EXERCISES

Some illustrations were offered indirectly earlier in this section in the course of defining the various types of dramatic and rhythmic exercises. More illustrations utilized in the development of specific concepts and generalizations follow.

One particular teacher in the fifth grade was explaining to her class that before Congress acts upon proposed legislation, it conducts hearings to learn as much as possible about the need for the law and the benefits it can bring to the people. This is in accordance with the basic principle from Political Science which states that, "In a democracy, government is the servant of the people; people are not the servants of the government. Government is by right an institution made by man for man. The source of authority resides in the people." The teacher asked the children to pretend that they were the Congress and that the President has just proposed an increase in taxes. How would they go about conducting hearings and what people would they call as witnesses? What would be some of the questions which they should ask these witnesses? After careful planning, the class proceeded with the enactment of the hearings. It proved to be a very interesting and rewarding experience.

Hoping to lead the children to the understanding of the same principle, a second-grade teacher was trying to convince the children that we pay taxes in order to support a government which should serve us. In a series of lessons she identified with the children and talked about the duties of the various government agents at the local level. She brought up specific instances in which children in the class have received assistance from government agents. Teacher and children working together listed a number of hypothetical situations in which government agents could be of assistance. Following these lessons and on the basis of what they learned, the teacher asked several youngsters to play the tax collector trying to convince a citizen why he had an obligation to pay his taxes.

In a particular fourth grade in connection with the generalization, "The recognition of human rights and human dignity is basic to personal relationships and to government," two children were chosen to dramatize a situation in which a white restaurant owner refuses service to a Negro. Their spontaneous arguments, based on the study of real situations, put them immediately in opposition to each other. Who was right and who was wrong? A lively discussion lasted for quite some time.

SUMMARY

Current events and dramatic and rhythmic exercises constitute additional resource areas for the teaching of social studies.

Current events have been defined as emerging social realities which effect social institutions. They assist in keeping the contemporary scene in focus as well as in bridging the gap between the classroom and the outside world. The utilization of current events has taken several forms. In some schools current events are taught separately while in others they have dominated the social studies program. The best way to utilize current events is to use them as means through which to supplement and enrich social studies instruction.

There is a variety of specific activities and resources of which the teacher can take advantage. These are presented along with specific illustrations to show how current events can be used in the development of concepts and generalizations. The section on current events ends with the suggestion that controversial issues play an important part in social studies and that they should not be neglected by the elementary school.

Dramatic and rhythmic exercises are activities which appeal to the elementary school child and the teacher should be careful to use them only if and when they contribute to the enrichment of social studies instruction.

Dramatics and rhythm, like most other resources, assist in developing an interest in and deeper understanding of social studies, as well as in providing opportunities for the teacher to vary instruction and evaluate the pupils. There are certain guidelines which the teacher should keep in mind. This chapter deals with these guidelines among the most important of which is stressing authenticity.

The chapter ends with a list of resources for the teacher and a number of illustrations to show how dramatization and rhythm can be used to develop concepts and generalizations.

Effective Evaluation Techniques in Social Studies

9

Effective Evaluation Techniques in
Social Studies

The quality of the total social studies program depends to a great extent on the quality of evaluation. The purpose of this chapter is to accomplish two things: first, to elaborate on the evaluation of pupil progress by presenting a number of guidelines and describing the various techniques of pupil evaluation; second, to emphasize the importance of constantly evaluating the entire social studies program and to suggest ways of keeping it up-to-date and related to the children's needs.

A. Evaluation of pupil progress

Schools, teachers and programs exist for the purpose of guiding children towards the achievement of well defined educational goals. The extent to which children progress towards these goals determines not only the amount of education that each pupil has received, but the quality and effectiveness of specific schools, teachers and programs as well. It can be said, therefore, that evaluating pupil progress is the central focus of all educational evaluation. Following are a number of basic principles to assist the social studies teacher in the evaluation of pupil progress:

1. *Evaluation should be based on the growth of all children, rather than on set standards.* In some countries and sometime ago in the United States, evaluation of pupil progress consisted simply of determining whether a particular child had reached the standards desired for a specific grade. Those children who met the standards were promoted while the others were not. In most cases the children kept back were eventually thrown out of school. As a result, many societies have been divided into two distinct classes, one educated and the other, usually the majority, uneducated. If one were to visit a country in which this system prevails, he would find that communication between the uneducated masses and the educated minority is virtually nonexistent. A country which lacks communication between important segments of its population is usually not far from civil strife.

The grade standard approach to evaluation ignores the conditions which might have caused a child to fall short of meeting the standards. It also ignores recent research findings which indicate that children do not benefit by simply repeating a grade. Let us not forget that children in the first grade, for instance, come from a variety of home experiences and backgrounds. Because of this some of them have only a little to learn in order to meet first-grade standards. Others who come from culturally deprived homes have a great deal more to learn. At the end of first grade, the children in the former group are promoted while many of the children in the latter group are not, in spite of the fact that some of them may have actually learned more that was new to them than did some of the seemingly more successful pupils. A child with potential is psychologically hurt when he is not promoted.

In the light of this, it can be seen that an evaluation based on the growth of each child is to be recommended. The teacher should assess the background, the potentialities, the abilities, and the weaknesses of each child and determine an expected achievement for each one of them. In this way the teacher would know not only how much to expect from each pupil, but what to do to advance his progress as well. Advocating the growth approach in evaluation should not give rise to the idea that there should be no standards, because not having standards means not having goals and purposes. What is advocated here is an approach which will help the children move forward and avoid the harm caused by non-promotion. The non-graded school and the various ways of grouping pupils reflect evaluation based on growth.

2 *Evaluation should be based on objectives the attainments of which are indicated by specific behaviors rather than on broad and vague statements.* In the first chapter, objectives were defined as changes in the cognitive, affective and psychomotor domains of the child. Unless the teacher is clear as to what the desired specific changes are, there can be no evaluation. Stating that the understanding of a concept or generalization is the objective, is not enough. Concepts and generalizations must be broken down into very specific behaviors. What will the child be able to do if he understood a particular concept or generalization? How would he behave if he developed a certain attitude? The answers to these questions will eliminate the vagueness of broad statements and will provide the teacher with clear-cut situations which can be evaluated.

3. *Evaluation should be balanced.* In the past, evaluation was heavily oriented towards objectives of a cognitive nature. But if social studies is to develop good citizens, knowledge is not enough. Success in elementary social studies means the development of certain commitments, attitudes and skills along with the acquisition of a body of knowledge. It is true that cognitive objectives are easier to evaluate, but this should not be an excuse for neglecting the evaluation of attitudes and skills.

4. *Evaluation is an integral part of instruction.* If we were to define instruction on the basis of what was written in this book, we could say that it is the involvement of children in designed and redesigned learning activities for the attainment of predetermined educational objectives. In other words, the first steps a teacher must take are to set objectives and design learning activities for the children. Then she involves the children in these activities. If the activities are appropriate the children will reach the objectives. If the activities are not appropriate, the teacher must redesign them. It is the information supplied by evaluation which dictates the redesigning of activities, and in this respect evaluation becomes an integral part of instruction.

5. *Evaluation is a continuous process.* Considering evaluation an integral part of instruction suggests that a teacher should not wait until the end of the lesson, the unit, or the semester to evaluate. Some of the questions which she should always be asking herself are: Did I make myself clear? Is this model good for the level of my children? Why did they not respond to my questions? Why did they not accept this or that assignment with enthusiasm? How many children developed the desired behavior? Shall I continue or should I try a different approach? Continuous evaluation is the method with which to avoid wasting valuable time.

6. *Evaluation should be done cooperatively.* A thorough evaluation of a child requires a careful examination of his behavior in as many situations as possible. The school represents only one of these situations; the home, the playground, the church or synagogue and the various children's clubs represent other situations. If the social studies program is successful, the qualities of good citizenship should be manifested in all of these situations. The teacher should seek the cooperation of parents, religious leaders, playground supervisors and club directors in order to achieve a complete and well rounded evaluation of the children. The teacher must be familiar with the community and with the children's lives outside school. In chapter 6 community resources were emphasized and mention was made of the value of having the teacher live in the community rather than commute. The concept of cooperative evaluation gives another reason for the teacher's being a part of the community in which she teaches.

Cooperative evaluation should be expanded to include the children as well. Because of the importance of the children's involvement in the evaluation process, the following separate guideline is offered:

7. *Self-evaluation should be encouraged.* Good teaching requires that the children internalize the purposes of instruction. When this is done the children tend to feel the need to evaluate themselves. In order for self-evaluation to develop there is a need for a non-threatening atmosphere. Evaluation should not be looked upon as the whip in the hands of the teacher to make the children work. It should be looked upon as the cooperative venture of teachers and pupils in assessing learning experiences and determining their value in terms of pupil progress towards objectives. Summarizing lessons with the children and cul-

minating activities in unit teaching situations are good examples of cooperative evaluation in which self-evaluation plays an important role. In order for self-evaluation to become possible the objectives must be well defined and clearly understood by the children.

8. *Evaluation should be done in a variety of ways.* Pencil-and-paper tests should not be the only or the predominant way of evaluating pupils. Pencil-and-paper tests are geared mostly toward cognitive objectives. Attitudes, commitments and skills are just as important. It is true that cognitive objectives are easier to evaluate, but evaluation could be made more comprehensive through the use of a variety of methods. A description of these methods will help clarify this approach.

TYPES AND TECHNIQUES OF EVALUATION

Evaluation can be classified in two types. One of them is more formal and occurs at a specified time and place. It is seen as a test situation by the person being evaluated and it consists of a set of uniform tasks for all persons tested. Usually the results of a formal testing situation can be expressed in quantitative terms. By contrast, there is the informal type of evaluation which extends over an indefinite period of time, is based upon situations which vary from person to person and is not perceived as a test by the person being evaluated. It is appropriate at this point to discuss the instruments and techniques used in each of these two types of evaluation.

Formal evaluation. Standardized tests and the various teacher-made tests are instruments of formal evaluation. An examination of a rather complete listing of standardized tests in social studies compiled by Barbara Peace[1] reveals that there are very few for the elementary grades. For the primary grades there are practically none. Here is a list of tests which can be used in the elementary grades:

1. *American School Achievement Tests: Part 4, Social Studies and Science.* Grades 4–6. Bobbs-Merrill Co., Inc., Indianapolis, Indiana.

2. *California Tests in Social Studies and Related Sciences.* Grades 4–8. California Test Bureau, Del Monte Research Park, Monterey, California.

---

[1] Barbara A. Peace, "Bibliography of Social Studies Tests," in: Harry D. Berg, ed., *Evaluation in Social Studies.* Thirty-fifth Yearbook, the National Council for the Social Studies (Washington, D. C.: NCSS, 1965), pp. 230–247.

3. *Geography Test. Municipal Tests: National Achievement Tests.* Grades 3–6, 6–8. Psychometric Affiliates, Chicago, Illinois.

4. *Geography Test: National Achievement Tests.* Grades 6–8. Psychometric Affiliates, Chicago, Illinois.

5. *Greig Social Studies Test.* Grades 6–8. Scholastic Testing Service, Inc., Bensenville, Illinois.

6. *History and Civics Tests: National Achievement Tests.* Grades 3–6, 6–8. Psychometric Affiliates, Chicago, Illinois.

7. *Iowa Tests of Basic Skills.* Grades 3–9. Houghton Mifflin Company, Boston, Massachusetts.

8. *Metropolitan Achievement Tests: Social Studies.* Grades 5–6. Harcourt, Brace and World, Inc., New York, New York.

9. *SRA Achievement Series.* Science Research Associates, Chicago, Illinois.

10. *Sequential Tests of Education Progress: Social Studies.* Grades 4–6. Educational Testing Service, Princeton, New Jersey.

11. *Social Studies Tests: National Achievement Tests.* Grades 4–6. Psychometric Affiliates, Chicago, Illinois.

12. *Stanford Achievement Test: Intermediate and Advanced Social Studies.* Grades 5–9. Harcourt, Brace and World, Inc., New York, N. Y.

13. *Tests of Critical Thinking in the Social Studies.* Bureau of Publications, Teachers College, Columbia University, New York, N. Y.

Before a standardized test is given, the teacher should examine it carefully to familiarize herself with its content and to make sure that the test covers the key learnings of the children for whom it is intended. Also, the teacher should determine whether the test's level of difficulty is appropriate. Furthermore, she should try to find out what kind of population was used to develop the norms of the test. If the results are to be meaningful, the teacher should know the kinds of children with whom she compares her class. Finding out that a class scored above the norms is not necessarily a cause for complacency. In potential, a particular class might stand well above the population used to derive the norms. In most cases norms represent the performance of the average child.

For detailed descriptions and evaluations on the above listed tests the teacher should refer to the following two sources which should be in the possession of every school:

1. Buros, Oscar K., ed., *The Sixth Mental Measurements Yearbook.*
   (Highland Park, New Jersey: The Gryphon Press, 1965).
   For some tests the teacher may have to refer to previous Mental
   Measurements Yearbooks.
2. Buros, Oscar K., ed., *Tests in Print: A Comprehensive Biblio-
   graphy of Tests for Use in Education, Psychology and Industry.*
   (Highland Park, New Jersey: The Gryphon Press, 1961).

Teacher-made tests consist of the objective or short-answer test,
and the essay test. The categories of the objective test are:

1. true—false
2. matching
3. completion
4. multiple-choice

It is not an easy task to construct a test. The first thing a teacher
must do is to determine the main concepts and understandings as
well as the skills on which the children must be tested. Then begins
the writing of the test items. Thorndike and Hagen cite the following
general maxims to be followed in writing test items:

1. Keep the reading difficulty of test items low.
2. Do not lift a statement verbatim from the book.
3. If an item is based on opinion or authority indicate whose
   opinion or what authority.
4. In planning a set of items for a test, take care that one item does
   not provide cues to the answer of another item or items.
5. Avoid the use of interlocking or interdependent items.
6. In a set of items, let the occurrence of correct responses follow
   essentially a random pattern.
7. Avoid trick and catch questions.
8. Try to avoid ambiguity of statement and meaning.
9. Beware of items dealing with trivia.[2]

An undisputed value of the objective test is the fact that it can
be scored easily. However, objective tests have been criticized for not
having the power to elicit and evaluate some of the most important
aspects of the child's potential such as his ability to generalize, to inter-

---

[2] Robert L. Thorndike, and Elizabeth Hagen, *Measurement and Evaluation in
Psychology and Education.* Second edition (New York: John Wiley and Sons, Inc.,
1965), pp. 61–65.

pret, to analyze, to synthesize and to evaluate. It is mainly through the essay test that these qualities can be tested and evaluated.

The following guidelines should direct the teacher in the construction and use of essay tests:

1. The questions should represent clearly defined objectives.
2. The format of the question should vary with the purpose of the question. All essay questions do not have to start with the usual commands: discuss, explain, describe. . . .
3. While constructing the questions, outline the expected acceptable answers. This outline can be used as the standard against which to grade the test as well as a means to avoid writing vague questions.
4. Determine the degree to which the pupil should be restricted in his response. Questions with too much freedom are difficult to grade.
5. Make sure the questions can be answered in the time allocated.
6. Try to make the examination more comprehensive by constructing shorter questions rather than a few long questions.
7. Children should be informed of the ground rules such as the points each question is worth and the time limit.
8. The same standards should be used for all children. Avoid being influenced by such factors as personality and handwriting. One way to achieve this is by constantly reviewing the standards and by covering the names of the students until the reading of all papers is completed.

Informal evaluation. The procedures of informal evaluation include rating scales, checklists, anecdotal records, discussion, observation, conferences with pupils and parents, and examination of samples of children's work. There are two basic reasons why informal evaluation is worthwhile. It makes possible evaluation of the two domains other than the cognitive, especially the affective, which cannot be subjected to the techniques of formal evaluation. One can test a class of youngsters to see how well they know the Bill of Rights, but he cannot test them to find out the degree to which they are committed to and respect these rights. Evaluation of children's commitments, values, dispositions, and democratic behavior cannot take place in a formal setting. Each child has to be evaluated on an individual basis and informally, in every life situation that the teacher can possibly observe.

The second reason for informal evaluation is that it is probably the only form of evaluation which can take place in the primary grades. As was pointed out, there are practically no standardized tests for the primary grades. Pencil-and-paper tests do not always give reliable results due to the reading difficulty which many children have at the primary level.

Informal evaluation is not easy. It requires knowledge of the child and the way of life which he leads in his environment. It requires planning in terms of defining specific goals and deciding on the specific procedures to be used. The procedures of rating and checking require the use of well planned forms. In rating scales, specific behaviors are broken down to more detailed behaviors which are placed on a continuum. The various sub-behaviors are clearly defined and usually are assigned numbers. In a checklist, clusters of behaviors are placed in a vertical list and the teacher simply checks whether they are present or not. Sometimes the form requires the teacher to indicate a degree of development of the specific behaviors, but this is done in a very subjective manner without referring to any sub-behaviors in an orderly continuum as in the rating scales. Some teachers construct rating scales and checklists in cooperation with the pupils, and the children use them for self-evaluation.

When discussion and observation are used to evaluate pupils, the teacher should be very clear in her objectives. Occasionally it is advisable to intensively observe certain children. Information collected should be written with care. Vocabulary should be chosen thoughtfully to make sure that a notation is not liable to misinterpretation. Terms such as "misbehaving," "aggressive," and "industrious" should be avoided because they do not mean the same thing to everyone, largely because they are not sufficiently specific. The teacher ought to be especially careful in the choice of words in writing anecdotal records. Summaries of behaviors of pupils written on little cards cannot mean much unless they are clearly and objectively written. Although these notes will be used for evaluation, they should themselves be descriptive rather than evaluative. The description should be factual, not interpretive; precise, not general.

This section would not be complete without some mention of sociograms. Sociograms are used to reveal information about the personal-social adjustment of pupils. The children are asked to list in order of preference the three persons in the class with whom they would most like to work on a project. Then, the sociogram is constructed by drawing a kind of map which shows by means of names and lines the choices of each pupil. It should be remembered that a sociogram shows the social interaction of a class at a particular time only. To get a clear picture, several sociograms should be made at different times and a variety of questions should be used. Teachers should emphasize that the pupils' choices will be confidential. Some teachers spend a good deal of time making sociograms look like art masterpieces. This is not necessary because they are not for display.

B. Evaluation of social studies programs

Evaluation of pupil progress is based on the assumption that there is a valid program with well defined objectives and sound content taught to reflect the most recent advances in Learning Psychology. A valid program, however, cannot be taken for granted and, once considered valid, it cannot long continue to be valid. There is a need for a continual evaluation of the program to make sure of the children's progress towards the proper objectives through the study of the most appropriate content and through involvement in pedagogically sound experiences. It is time teachers took the situation in their own hands so that mistakes of the past can be avoided. For too long we have been content with a program full of deficiencies. (For a description of the deficiencies refer to chapter 2.)

Following are some major steps which teachers, in committee and individually, can follow in order to maintain a good program:

1. *Revise the program according to the most current social trends and realities.* Our world changes very rapidly and, one could say, in a very substantial way. Teachers should be cognizant of this and keep revising the social studies program accordingly. Just a little over ten years ago, Stanley Dimond[3] wrote a very useful article on this theme. He pointed out the significance of social-trend analysis and elucidated the implica-

---

[3] Stanley E. Dimond, "Current Social Trends and Their Implications for the Social-Studies Program," in: Nelson B. Henry, ed., *Social Studies in the Elementary School*. Fifty-Sixth Yearbook, the National Society for the Study of Education, Part II (Chicago: The University of Chicago Press, 1957), pp. 48–75.

tions of this analysis for the social studies program. Professor Dimond argues that social-trend analysis makes the following four definite contributions to teaching the social studies in the elementary school:

1. Objectives are initiated and verified.
2. The neglect of important content areas is avoided.
3. The interests of pupils and teachers are enlarged.
4. Variety in method is encouraged.

Dr. Dimond analyzed and desscribed the social trends in this fashion:

1. World Political Trends:
   a. The Ideological Struggle
   b. War and the Threats of War
2. Economic and Technological Trends:
   a. The Status of Raw Materials in the United States
   b. Power Resources
   c. Economic Controls
   d. Automation
   e. Transportation and Communication
3. Societal Trends:
   a. Population
   b. Health
   c. Leisure
   d. Integrity
   e. The School

The questions which should be raised now by each teacher are: What is the status of the world at the present time in terms of the above outline? Does the outline itself need any revision due to new developments? This step in the evaluation of the social studies program demands that the teacher be a student of the world in which we live.

2. *Revise the program on the basis of current findings about children.* It was pointed out earlier that much of the content in present elementary social studies is below the level of interest and sophistication of today's children. Realizing the great effect which mass media have had upon children should alone indelibly impress this fact.

3. *Revise the program on the basis of what is considered to be sound pedagogical methodology.* For centuries children played the role of passive listeners in the learning process. Their only active involvement was

memorizing. Now we recognize that in order for learning to take place the children must assume a more active role in the learning process. We also recognize that while the accumulation of knowledge is important, it is equally important, if not more important, to develop the thinking power of the child. To accomplish this we must depart from a descriptive program and implement a program conducive to problem solving. The teacher should always ask herself. Does my program provide enough opportunities for the children to identify social problems and reflect upon them? Unfortunately social studies programs thus far have followed the "guided tour" approach excessively.

4. *Revise the program according to present trends in social studies education.* The majority of these trends have already been elaborated, especially in Chapters 2, 3 and 4. The more important ones are simply listed:

    a. More emphasis on structure as compared to the programs which were oriented towards "social learnings"; that is, more emphasis on developing concepts and generalizations identified by social scientists.

    b. More emphasis on the interdisciplinary approach.

    c. More emphasis on the use of primary resources and a variety of instructional resources as contrasted with the use of one textbook.

    d. An effort to provide for a balance between the study of the western and non-western worlds

    e. An effort to study each culture not in isolation, but within the context of the rest of the world.

    f. More emphasis on the development of intellectual (problem solving) skills.

    g. An effort to provide for a balance between cognitive, affective, and skill objectives.

5. *Be ready to revise the program on the basis of evaluations of pupil progress.* It has already been stated that a program is beneficial if it helps pupils to reach certain objectives. If it is discovered, through pupil progress evaluation, that children fall short of reaching the objectives, the program might need revision in certain ways. Industry has a system of evaluation which they call "quality control." If it is discovered that products do not meet set standards, a careful study is made of the plant system and attempts made to improve it. More of this needs to be done in education. Some have recently been wondering whether the

social studies program really develops worthwhile societal behaviors in the individuals who graduate from our schools.

SUMMARY

Evaluation is of paramount importance to the social studies. Pupil progress should be evaluated as should be the program itself. A number of guidelines have been presented to assist the teacher in developing a theoretical framework for the evaluation of pupil progress.

Evaluation can be undertaken formally or informally. Formal evaluation takes place at a specified time and place and is uniform for all pupils. It is seen by the pupils as a test situation. Standardized tests and teacher-made tests represent the two types of formal evaluation. There is a tendency for formal evaluation to be concerned primarily with cognitive learnings.

Informal evaluation extends over an indefinite period of time. It is more valuable for the elementary school, especially for the primary grades where formal evaluation of young children is difficult. Informal evaluation involves such techniques as rating, checklists, anecdotal records, discussion, observation, conferences with pupils and parents, and examination of samples of children's work.

Pupil progress should be based on a sound program, and this program cannot be taken for granted. It is essential that the social studies program be subjected to constant evaluation and revision on the basis of emerging social realities, new findings on the nature of children, and advances in teaching methodology.

Guidelines for Administrators and Teachers

10

Guidelines for Administrators and Teachers

A study was conducted by Donald Lee Schilson[1] to identify and classify problems encountered by beginning teachers in elementary social studies. Teachers as well as supervisors were asked to respond to a number of questions. Some of the problems which the teachers listed were:

1. Shortage of interesting and graded supplementary materials
2. Lack of curriculum guides
3. Textbooks too easy
4. Shortage of films and filmstrips
5. Lack of television and radio for special programs
6. Lack of suitable maps, globes and pictures
7. Difficulty in considering the individual differences because of large classes
8. Lack of information concerning community resources

---

[1] Donald Lee Schilson, "Problems of Beginning Teachers in Elementary Social Studies," *Dissertation Abstracts.* Volume 23 (November 1962), p. 1561.

The administrators stated the teacher's problems as follows:

1. Ignoring sources outside the textbook
2. Lack of knowledge concerning the selection and use of suplementary materials
3. Poorly illustrating bulletin boards
4. Trouble working with groups

It is rather interesting to note that teachers see many of their problems in terms of lack of proper conditions, facilities and materials. At the same time, administrators view the same problems in terms of the teacher's lack of ability or application. In other words, both teachers and administrators blame the other for the undeniable problems which exist. In view of this, the first general recommendation to teachers and administrators is to stop blaming each other and join forces in order to work towards the improvement of the program. This is an urgent matter and the purpose of this chapter is to offer specific suggestions to help form a common ground upon which both groups may rally.

Suggestions to administrators

1. *Provide an atmosphere which will allow the teachers to see the need for and take the initiative in curriculum improvement.* Pronouncements about curriculum development and revision which come exclusively from the administration are not likely to produce the desired results. Teachers work best on curriculum not when they are told to do so, but when they feel the need. If there is a need for curriculum improvement and the teachers do not see it, it is the job of the administrator to develop an awareness of this need through indirect methods rather than through edicts. If the situation continues unchanged, it would be more advisable to look for new teachers rather than to compel the present ones.

2. *Provide the teachers with the flexibility needed to be creative.* Each classroom presents a unique situation and the teachers should not be expected to follow a rigid program. If a teacher is convinced that she can do a better job teaching without a textbook, she should be allowed to do so regardless of what the related ruling of the school board may be. Scheduling should also be flexible. Learning activities are of first priority in the planning of the schedule, not lunch, routine health

activities, announcements, and the like. Let us not forget that learning is the primary responsibility of the school. Everything else is designed to facilitate the learning process.

3. *See that the school builds a good library and has it open for the children at all times.* There is no excuse for any school not having a good library for the children. The federal government is presently allocating considerable amounts of money for this purpose. Getting a library is one thing, using it properly is another. There are cases in which libraries stay closed most of the time, each class being allowed one hour a day or only twice a week. Many librarians tend to be overly protective of the books, and the children hesitate to borrow them because they are afraid that they might not be able to keep them in perfect condition. Books are to be used and worn out. It should be expected that some of them will get lost.

4. *In addition to an adequate library, see that the teachers get other types of materials which they need.* Several chapters in this book were devoted to the various types of materials and their importance in the teaching of social studies. Make sure the teachers obtain these materials. A film, for example, is only of benefit if it can be used at the proper time in connection with the development of a particular unit.

5. *Support the teachers in the treatment of controversial issues.* Controversial issues have a place in the elementary school. Many teachers, however, hesitate to teach controversial issues because of fear it might cause conflict with some parents. This has happened many times with many teachers losing their jobs. The administrator should protect the teacher and find ways of enlightening the public in regard to the treatment of controversial issues.

6. *Do not use faculty meetings to make announcements.* Announcements should be mimeographed and distributed; the meetings should be turned over to the teachers for professional matters. Social studies is in ferment and there is much to be brought to the attention of the teachers for implementation.

7. *Be a colleague to the teachers.* Administrators who consistently assume an attitude of superiority or refer to the faculty as "my teachers" are not apt to promote good morale. Educating children is a common responsibility for both teachers and administrators. Both groups are

professionals. They should work in a spirit of cooperation, not in an atmosphere of threat and insecurity.

8. *Administrators should keep abreast of new developments in social studies.*

Suggestions to teachers

Although this book is a series of suggestions for teachers, this section of it concentrates on suggested personal improvements.

1. *Try to develop a philosophical point of view as a social studies teacher.* Do you teach social studies because you strongly believe in what you are trying to accomplish? Flssisting pupils to funtion well in contemporary society should be your ultimate aim.

2. *Study to understand world events.* A deep personal desire to understand the curse of world events is indispensable. Read as much as you can in all fields of social sciences and do not hesitate to venture into analysis of what you read. In planning a master's program or when you simply go back for refresher studies, take some social science courses. Especially take courses which touch upon the major problems of our society such as Urban Geography, Minority Groups in the United States, the Labor Movement, and the like. Do not limit yourself to Education courses only.

While you are taking the substantive courses, make sure you obtain from them what you need as a teacher. Ask the professor to formulate a limited number of generalizations. Use these generalizations to evaluate your program and determine whether it is accurate and up-to-date. Submit teaching units which you have developed, and ask the professor to evaluate the concepts and generalizations which you have selected for development.

3. *Keep in mind that you are an expert in teaching.* When it comes to teaching, everyone thinks he knows how to do it best and is ready with advice for the teacher. They forget that the teacher has studied for years in order to learn how to teach and that she has a wealth of firsthand experience. Stand up for your professional rights, but first make sure that you have developed your professional stature and know how to defend intelligently that for which you stand.

4. *Travel as much as you can.* Travelling is one of the most enriching experiences. If you can afford to go to Europe or Latin America or

any other part of the world, do so. But there are also places very close which you can visit without much expense. If you are teaching in a rural area, visit the nearest large city and observe situations related to what you are teaching the youngsters. Visit ports, slum areas, suburbs, industrial areas, museums, and historical places. Artists are noted for perceiving most of what they see from an artistic point of view. Teachers should develop a teacher's viewpoint, in essence—intellectual curiosity.

5. *Open your classroom and even your house to foreign visitors.* Some foreign visitors might not appear to have anything to offer directly to children. Get to know them anyway. Much can be learned in informal conversations with them.

6. *Join various professional organizations.* The most important organization for social studies teachers is the National Council for the Social Studies. Many teachers do not even know that this organization exists. Membership dues are $9.00 and this covers subscription to *Social Education* as well as the Yearbook. *Social Education* is published every month through the academic year and contains articles of a substantive nature, others on methodology, book reviews, listings of films and other aids and features.

7. *Join civic and community organizations.* Ours is the age of groups. It is difficult for someone to understand and participate in society unless he is a member of various groups. It is within these groups that the teacher can learn the dynamics of community life.

8. *Try new methods advocated in research articles.* In view of the ferment that is taking place in the social studies, there is a considerable amount of research taking place. Teachers are urged not only to read it, but also to try in their classrooms some of the new methods recommended. Do not hesitate to depart from routine. The result most likely to occur is the children's becoming excited about social studies.

9. *Listen to consultants and seriously consider their advice, but do not allow them to dictate what you should do.* This suggestion is concerned mainly with outside consultants, but it does not exclude the regular social studies consultants wherever they exist. Consultants are good to answer questions and provide stimulation. They should work with the teachers in developing a general framework of operation. The details within

the classroom should be the duty of the teacher. The teacher usually knows best how to work effectively with her particular group of children.

Summary

Administrators and teachers must see themselves as colleagues and work together for the common purpose of educating the children. Several suggestions were made in this chapter to both groups with the hope of aiding in the improvement of their professional stature. It is entirely possible that a strengthened social studies program will contribute towards a better understanding among people and to the elimination of some of the major evils which plague our society.

Index

Index